Guide Dogs of America

A HISTORY

Patrick S. Halley

ISBN: 1-4774-3228-0

ISBN-13: 978-1477432280

Library of Congress Control Number: 2012908633

Visit Amazon.com to order additional copies

Design by AP Associates

Original photography by Bill Burke, Page One Photography

Patrick S. Halley

Patrick S. Halley is the author of *On the Road with Hillary* (Viking, 2002), and *Wimpy* (Kelly Press 2008).

He spent nine years doing advance for Hillary Rodham Clinton. He was Executive Director of the Massachusetts Democratic Party and worked as an advance man or state director in six presidential campaigns. Prior to that he had a career in law enforcement, serving as chief of operations for both the Attorney General of Massachusetts and the Middlesex County District Attorney.

He lives in Massachusetts and Florida.

For the Geppners

– I came among you,
and you took me in.

Foreword

R. Thomas Buffenbarger

International President International Association of Machinists and Aerospace Workers

When I was in grade school, my father, a member of the IAM, would let me read the weekly newspaper he received from his union. Like many kids, I was fond of dogs and I was surprised to see them featured so prominently in *The Machinist*. My father explained that these were not just any dogs, they were guide dogs for the blind, and his union helped provide them free of charge to people who had lost their sight. He also explained with great pride that International Guiding Eyes – now known as Guide Dogs of America – the organization that trained these marvelous animals, was started by a machinist. This was *our* project, *our* charity, and *our* union was fully committed to its success.

The relationship between the IAM and Guide Dogs of America goes back to the very founding of the organization. When Joseph Jones had the idea of starting a school to provide guide dogs, he needed money and organizational support to make that dream a reality. He turned to his union and, in 1946 the Executive Council of the IAM officially recognized International Guiding Eyes and put the full strength of nearly half a million members at his disposal. Brothers and sisters from across the United States and Canada immediately embraced this as our signature charity because it captures the very spirit of trade union solidarity: where we look out for our own and do everything we possibly can to help those in society who are less fortunate.

IAM members rolled up their sleeves and began raising funds in every conceivable way to help Joseph Jones' school grow and prosper. From small talent shows in New York and Los Angeles in the 1940's to golf tournaments, car shows, trap shoots, raffles, the sale of calendars, "Hawgs for Dawgs" motorcycle runs, and an annual fundraising dinner in Las Vegas that now brings in more than a million dollars, our members have provided unwavering support.

We are thrilled that Guide Dogs of America is now recognized globally as one of the finest schools of its kind. The fact that so many people hold Guide Dogs of America in such esteem and provide it so much respect not only validates our efforts, it makes us want to do even more to ensure its continued success.

The commitment of the IAM to Guide Dogs of America is just as strong today as it has been since the day Joseph Jones, aided only by a white cane, made his pitch to the Executive Council.

We are proud to call this *our* project, *our* charity, and *our union* will see to its success for many generations to come.

Yours in Solidarity

R. Thomas Buffenbarger
International President

Contents

Introduction
Dale E. Hartford
President, Guide Dogs of America

Since it was founded as International Guiding Eyes in 1948, Guide Dogs of America has provided more than three thousand scientifically trained canine partners to visually impaired people from the United States and Canada.

It began with Joseph Jones, who in 1942 was denied a guide dog because he was deemed too old, at fifty-seven, to work successfully with a canine partner. Jones refused to accept that assessment and turned to his union, the International Association of Machinists, for help. With the union's full support behind him Jones began his own journey that resulted in the modern, successful and vibrant organization we have today.

This is the story of how we breed, train and deploy guide dogs. It's the story of puppy raisers, professional trainers, scientists, veterinarians and our professional staff who work with these carefully screened dogs. It's the story of thousands of people who raise money, hold events, advocate for the rights of the visually impaired and build the tremendous public support we enjoy. And it's also the story of families, Hollywood personalities, and a very special union and its members who have given generously of their time, talents and funds.

It is only with a thorough understanding of our history that we can make sound decisions about our future. The future of GDA is bright because of the dedication of hundreds of people who continue to give generously in many ways. We are extremely fortunate to have volunteers and staff who raise the money, raise the puppies and just as importantly, raise awareness of the needs of the visually impaired and how Guide Dogs of America can help.

We're very proud of the remarkable story presented here about how the determination of a single visually impaired man led to an organization that has helped thousands of people lead a better life. We hope you enjoy learning a bit about our history and will become part of our future.

DALE E. HARTFORD
PRESIDENT, GUIDE DOGS OF AMERICA

PART I

History of Guide Dogs of America

"It seems like an impossible
task that I have undertaken.
I fully realize the proportions of
this undertaking, and none will
tell me that it can't be done."

(Joseph W. Jones, Sr.)

Chapter 1
The Guide Dog Movement

The year was 1916, and the German Army was advancing into France as World War I raged on. At a German Army field hospital near Soissons, a twenty-three-year-old officer named Lambert Kreimer, who had taken machine gun rounds to his chest, lay seriously wounded. Doctors gave the young man, a war hero who had been wounded six other times in previous battles and had received the Iron Cross Medal, Germany's highest military honor, very little chance of survival.

Blinded soldier Willie Reinstein, Lambert A. Kreimer, and Rolf, the world's first scientifically trained guide dog.

Kreimer, like his father and grandfather before him, had been a member of the green uniformed German Forestry Corps before the war, where he constantly worked with dogs. He had become fascinated with their desire to work on man's behalf. In his spare time he experimented with German Shepherd dogs, occasionally donning a blindfold and patiently urging them to guide him through the woods without running him into trees or other obstacles. Buoyed by a degree of success, he wrote an essay suggesting that dogs could be trained to lead the blind.

When the war started, the Forestry Corps members and their dogs were pressed into service. Kreimer was so adept at training canines that he was placed in charge of the German War Dog Program, where he rose through the ranks teaching dogs to perform sentry duty, deliver messages, and track scents. He was particularly interested in the notion that dogs could be used to find wounded soldiers on the battlefield to allow rescuers to get them to hospitals, a skill that may have saved his life when he was felled by several bullets to the left side of his chest.

As he lay on his hospital cot, medics brought in another wounded soldier named Willie Reinstein. His left eye was missing, and a bullet had torn through the bridge of his nose and destroyed his right eye. Reinstein would never again see daylight.

Gradually and against long odds, Kreimer and Reinstein began to recover and the two of them struck up a friendship. Kreimer suggested that he could train a dog they had seen scrounging around the hospital's garbage pails to guide the blind soldier. Reinstein, still in denial about the permanence of his condition, declined, telling Kreimer that he had no desire to be seen as a cripple being led around by a dog. One afternoon while returning from a walk on the hospital grounds, Reinstein miscounted the number of steps leading to the hospital door and took a sudden and painful fall to the gravel walk, loosening his stitches and reopening his wounds. Kreimer, awoken by the screams of his friend, hobbled to the door and saw Reinstein lying on the ground writhing in pain and bleeding.

Kreimer would later recall that it was at that moment that he vowed to devote his life to improving life for the blind by training dogs to serve as their guides. [1]

Reinstein was sufficiently shaken by the incident to agree to Kreimer's plan to train the camp dog, a small animal they named "Rolf." The two soldiers had a new mission, and over the next twenty-seven days they worked day and night to train Rolf how to lead Reinstein and developed a system of recognizable commands for Reinstein to use to let Rolf become his substitute eyes.

When the soldier and the dog, always working close to his master's left leg, demonstrated the ability to navigate the hospital grounds, including the stairs, without incident, Kreimer deemed his experiment a success.

When he was released from the hospital, Kreimer was assigned to the elite *Garde Du Corps*, the Kaiser's bodyguard detail. Kaiser Wilhelm II soon became fond of the businesslike Kreimer, who stood six feet two inches tall and was more than two hundred pounds of solid muscle. Despite his multiple war wounds, Kreimer managed to regain full strength and stay physically fit. A natural outdoorsman, Kreimer enjoyed hunting and was good at it. He accompanied the Kaiser on several hunting trips and impressed the leader of Germany with his keen instincts and excellent marksmanship.

When the time came for him to move on to another assignment, he requested that he be allowed to return to training dogs, a request the Kaiser was happy to grant. He gave Kreimer a rare three barrel shotgun as a parting gift, and instructed his military attaché to see to it that Kreimer was promoted to the rank of Captain and assigned to run a school the army was setting up at Oldenburg to train Shepherd dogs to guide soldiers blinded in the war. He would be teamed there with Doctor Gerhard Stalling, who would see to the medical needs of the students.

The trench warfare of the First World War, which included extensive use of poisonous gases, had left a considerable number of soldiers blinded. Stalling worked with the patients to remedy their physical ailments, while Kreimer worked to restore their mobility through the use of guide dogs.

Kreimer's initial efforts working with shepherd dogs were a success, and the army soon established branch schools in Bonn, Breslau, Dresden, Essen, Freiburg, Hamburg, Hanover Magdeburg, and Munster. By the end of the war the schools were training up to six hundred teams of guide dogs and students per year.

In 1919, the Treaty of Versailles ended the conflict between Germany and the allied powers, and led to severe economic depression. The army schools were shuttered in 1924, but were soon replaced by one large school in Potsdam, a cooperative effort between the Weimar Republic, the Shepherd Dog Club of

Germany and the Association of War Blinded Veterans. Kreimer was appointed Head Trainer, and he supervised a staff of 85 trainers drawn from the ranks of the schools he and Stalling had established. The Potsdam school operated on a much larger scale than the Army schools, training more than one hundred dogs at a time, and graduating at least a dozen teams a month. The school would operate for more than eighteen years and provide more than 2,500 fully trained guide dogs.

The American Guide Dog Movement began as a direct result of the success of the Germans at Potsdam. In 1927, three years after the Potsdam school was established, the *Saturday Evening Post* contacted an American expatriate, Dorothy Harrison Eustace, who was living in Switzerland and training dogs for police and army work and asked her to write a human interest story on dogs for their magazine. Eustace, from a prominent Philadelphia family, had adopted a German Shepherd puppy named "Hans" on a trip to Europe a few years earlier, and was so impressed with the dog's intelligence that when she and her husband relocated to a Swiss estate they named Fortunate Fields, she bought a litter of Shepherd puppies and established a training school of her own. She employed the services of a self-taught geneticist named Elliott "Jack" Humphrey, and before long they were churning out dozens of trained Shepherd dogs for police and army clients.

Eustace was concerned that if she wrote about her own experiences at Fortunate Fields, where business was already at capacity, the article might generate more demand than they could reasonably handle, so she proposed to her editors that she instead write about the school she and her husband had visited in Potsdam where dogs were being trained to assist the blind.

Eustace traveled to Potsdam in the summer of 1927, to interview trainers and take pictures. She submitted her story with the title: "The Seeing Eye," which she drew from a verse in the Old Testament (Proverbs 20:12: "The hearing ear and the seeing eye, the Lord has made them both."). *The Saturday Evening Post*

Dorothy Harrison Eustace's article in *The Saturday Evening Post* sparked American interest in the guide dog movement.

published it, accompanied by six photographs, on November 5, 1927. [2]

In the article, Eustace confessed her initial skepticism: "I had seen many so-called trained dogs which, put to the test, did mediocre work accompanied by many excuses that I was more or less prepared to hear reasons for poor work. I had expected possibly to see an instructor with eyes bandaged give an exhibition with one special dog to the running accompaniment of 'He's off his work today ---didn't eat this morning; he was not exercised yesterday; that's funny, he usually does that perfectly; there must be something distracting him; and so on --- all kinds of incidents that would go to prove my contention that, intelligent and as full of courage as this grand breed of dogs is, it is too much to ask of him to take the entire responsibility of a blind man's life." [3]

What she found, and related in her article, was quite the opposite. Kreimer had perfected the art of training dogs to guide the blind, and the Potsdam dogs were first rate. She described men arriving at the school "…forlorn, with lined, anxious faces and drooping bodies…" who, through the assistance of a guide dog were: "…remade; life takes on a new interest; shoulders lose their droop, backs straighten up and feet forget to shuffle." [4]

Eustace asked the school's administrative director, Mr. Liese, for permission to watch one student as he traveled off campus learning to work with his new guide dog, and offered a glowing account of what she witnessed: "I shall never forget the change that came over one man as he turned away from the gate. It was as though a complete transformation had taken place before my eyes. One moment it was the uncertain, shuffling blind man, tapping with a cane, the next it was an assured person, with his dog firmly in hand and his head up, who walked toward us quickly and firmly, giving his orders in a low confident voice. That one quick glimpse of the crying need for guidance and companionship in the lonely, all-enveloping darkness stood out clearly before my swimming eyes. To think that one small dog could stand for so much in the life of a human being, not only in his usual role of companion, but as his eyes, sword, and shield and buckler! How many humans could fill those roles with the same uncomplaining devotion and untiring fidelity? Darned few, I think." [5]

After explaining the extensive training regimen of dog and student, and recounting in more detail their ability to maneuver through the streets of Potsdam, Eustace closed with a paragraph that would ultimately help launch the guide dog movement in America:

"The future for all blind men can be the same, however blinded. No longer dependent on a member of the family, a friend or a paid attendant, the blind can once more take up their normal lives as nearly as possible where they left them off, and each can begin to go back to a wage-earning occupation, secure in the knowledge that he can get to and from his work safely and without cost; that crowds and traffic have no longer any terrors for him and that his evenings can be spent among friends without responsibility to burden them; and last, but far from least, that long, healthful walks are now possible to exercise off the unhealthy fat of inactivity and so keep the body strong and fit. Gentlemen, again without reservation, I give you the shepherd dog." [6]

Meanwhile, in the United States, a Russian immigrant in Saint Paul, Minnesota, had begun a program similar to Eustace's Fortunate Fields operation at his country estate in Minnetonka, about six miles west of Minneapolis. John L. Sinykin emigrated from Russia in 1906, and had established a booming wholesale cosmetics company. In addition to his business interests, Sinykin had a passion for dogs and had imported a few Shepherd dogs from Germany and was training them at his La Salle Kennels. He also established a foundation called Master Eye, with a notion of training his shepherds to lead the blind.

Sinykin learned of Kreimer's success at Potsdam, either through Eustace's article or elsewhere, and asked for his assistance in providing a guide dog to a United States Senator from Minnesota, Thomas Schall, who was legally blind. Kreimer complied, and sent a dog he had trained named "Lux," in 1927. The dog was renamed "Lux of La Salle," and presented to Senator Schall as a gift. Lux, having been trained in Germany, only understood commands in that language, and Captain Kreimer mailed instructions to the senator on how to use basic German words to get his canine guide to lead him through the streets of the nation's capital.

Lux was a big hit on Capitol Hill, and newspapers across the country carried a wire service story in January, 1928:

Blind Senator Has Friend and Guide Goes About Streets

Senator Thomas D. Schall, blind congressman from Minnesota, has a new friend who is an unerring guide when the senator goes about the capital transacting business. The friend is the German Police Dog who also sees that Senator Schall is protected. The task formerly was performed by a secretary. [7]

JANUARY 22, 1928.
SAINT PAUL PIONEER PRESS

SENATOR SCHALL'S NEW EYES AT WORK—Lux, the German police dog acquired recently by Minnesota's blind senator, guides him safely through traffic in Washington. They are shown here on the way to the Capitol.

Later that year, President Calvin Coolidge heard of the dog that was guiding a senator around the town and onto the floor of the senate, and invited the pair to the White House for a visit, an event that was also reported in newspapers nationwide.

Sees For His Master

When President Coolidge heard how Thomas Schall, blind senator from Minnesota, is led about by his dog, "Lux," he asked that the dog be brought to the White House for a visit. [8]

Lux paid that visit on Monday, December 7th, prompting President Coolidge, when asked about his guest to remark: "It was the first visitor I have had in over seven years that did not want anything."

The Guide Dog Movement was picking up steam in America. In addition to Sinykin's program at La Salle, a twenty-year-old blind man from Nashville, Tennessee contacted Dorothy Eustace four days after her article was published in *The Saturday Evening Post* to request a guide dog for himself and help setting up a school to train guide dogs. Morris Frank, who had been totally blind since age sixteen, begged Eustace for the chance to regain his independence with a guide dog.

"Is what you say really true?" Frank inquired. "If so, I want one of those dogs! And I am not alone. Thousands of blind like me abhor being dependent on others. Help me and I will help them. Train me and I will bring back my dog and show people here how a blind man can be absolutely on his own. We can then set up an instruction center in this country to give all those here who want it a chance at a new life." [9]

In her biography of Dorothy Harrison Eustace, *"Independent Vision,"* (Purdue University Press, 2010), author Miriam Ascarelli recounts what happened next: "Dorothy wrote back. She had never trained guide dogs for the blind, she told Morris, but if he had the courage to travel to Switzerland

for a dog, she would match him up with a dog and a qualified trainer, she said." [10]

Morris Frank responded enthusiastically and eventually made his way to Fortunate Fields, where he was introduced to head trainer Jack Humphrey. On Morris' second day in Switzerland, Humphrey gave Frank a small ball of hamburger and left the room. Frank later recalled hearing a dog's nails clicking on the floor.

"I held out the morsel, and while she accepted it with dignity, I knelt and patted her, stroking her soft silky coat." [11]

That shepherd dog, originally called "Kiss," but soon renamed "Buddy," was destined to become the most famous guide dog in American history.

Several weeks after he was paired with Buddy, Frank completed his training and was preparing to return to Nashville with hopes of establishing his own training school for guide dogs. He asked Dorothy Eustace to provide him with dogs, trainers and money to get the school up and running. She was receptive to the idea, but insisted that he had to fulfill two requirements before she would provide her support. First, he would have to demonstrate to the public that Buddy was capable of dealing with the hectic traffic of American cities. Then, Frank would have to begin the process of educating the American public to allow guide dogs into public spaces where dogs were typically forbidden entrance, such as trains, work places and restaurants.

Morris Frank and Buddy returned to the United States aboard ship, arriving in New York Harbor, in June, 1928, where a gaggle of reporters and photographers greeted them, the result of some behind the scenes encouragement from Dorothy Eustace. Frank was immediately put to the test of proving that Buddy was capable of handling the traffic of a major American city. One of the reporters on hand challenged Frank to cross West Street, among the city's busiest thoroughfares. Ascarelli described what happened next:

"Cars honked. Trucks sped by spewing exhaust. It was a traffic inferno. Buddy took a few steps forward, then stopped. A huge truck roared by. Buddy moved forward again. Then she stopped, backed up, and started again. Morris knew he had to put all of his faith in Buddy to guide him safely to the other side. Later he recalled: 'I shall never forget the next three minutes. Ten-ton trucks rocketing past, cabs blowing their horns in our ears, drivers shouting at us. One fellow yelled, 'You damn fool, do you want to get killed?'" [12]

While Morris Frank and Buddy were training at Fortunate Fields, John Sinykin was busy trying to get Captain Lambert Kreimer to leave Germany and come to America to run the La Salle Kennels. With the help of Senator Schall and the United States State Department, he was able to convince the German Government to let Kreimer out of his contract to run the school at Potsdam.

Kreimer and his wife Frances, who went by "Fanny," arrived in New York City on June 30, 1929, aboard the SS Munchen from Bremen, Germany. Kreimer brought four Shepherd Dogs with him from Germany, "Almo von Eckenweiler," "Melot von Mangolstein," Junkers von der Wolfshide," and "Kautz von Hain." [13]

Kreimer and Sinykin wasted little time in getting their guide dogs into the hands of blind recipients. They traveled to Los Angeles in mid-August, 1929, and presented "Almo" to author William A. Christensen. The Los Angeles Times was impressed enough by his visit to run a story on page two of their August 26, 1929, edition complete with a picture of a smiling Kreimer, "former member of the Kaiser's bodyguard." [14]

Kreimer trained dogs at La Salle until 1937, when he moved to Burbank, California, and established his own operation, which he called

"The Pioneer Training School for Guide Dogs." He became a United States citizen on May 9, 1941.

He had already been decorated by five different governments for his work training guide dogs for the blind, and he would soon add decorations from the United States for his work training dogs for the United States Army in World War II.

By the time the war started, the movement Kreimer had started from his hospital bed in Soissons was in full swing in America, with The Guiding Eye training dogs in New Jersey, La Salle training them in Minnesota, and Kreimer operating in California.

Unfortunately, the bloodiest conflict the world had seen to that time was about to inflict blindness on a record number of soldiers. But thanks to the efforts of Lambert Kreimer, John Sinykin and Morris Frank, the United States was advancing the Guide Dog Movement, providing scientifically trained German Shepherds to guide those who lost their vision.   ●

Morris Frank negotiates a city street with Buddy, the second guide dog to come to America.

Chapter 2
Joseph W. Jones

Meridian, Mississippi was established in 1860, and four years later General William Tecumseh Sherman burnt it to the ground in his "march to the sea." In those four short years Meridian had become a gem of the Confederacy, served by two railroads, the Mobile and Ohio and the Southern Railway. The Confederate Army had made Meridian a hub, with an arsenal, a military hospital and a prisoner of war stockade.

Sherman's destruction of the city included the railroad buildings, machine shops, turning table, 55 miles of railroad, 53 bridges, 6,075 feet of trestle work, 19 locomotives, 28 steam cars, and three saw mills. [1]

Reporting to his superiors, Sherman said: "100,000 men worked hard and with a will in that work of destruction, with axes, crowbars, and with fire, and I have no hesitation in pronouncing the work was well done. Meridian, with its depots, storehouses, arsenal, hospitals, offices, hotels and cantonments no longer exists." [2]

Meridian proved to be far more resilient than Sherman anticipated, and within twenty years of its destruction it had again become a booming metropolis, the largest city in Mississippi. It was there, in 1885, that Joseph and Mary Jones welcomed the first of their five children, a boy they named Joseph.

The Jones family made their home on Fifth Street, in a house they owned without a mortgage. Joseph was employed as a railroad blacksmith and Mary stayed at home with their children. [3]

At age eight young Joseph became seriously ill with what his doctor described as "tropical fever," and nearly died. He eventually recovered his health, but he lost his vision. [4]

Meridian, Mississippi, from a turn of the century postcard.

Joseph W. Jones delighted the delegates to the 1948 IAM Grand Lodge Convention with a little down-home humor from his days in Meridian, Mississippi, comparing the challenges he faced launching International Guiding Eyes with a story of some local renown:

"Like the old-timer down in Mississippi – and this part of a true story. It happened many years ago and if any of you delegates are from down around Meridian, you will recall it."

"Sam Leveran, a local man in Meridian, Mississippi, said he was going to run a railroad up to Meridian from Union, a distance of thirty miles. A lot of people in the section had never seen a locomotive at that time, and one old-timer read the announcement in the newspaper when it came out in the weekly issue of the Union paper, showing a picture of the locomotive. He said, 'Well, they're wasting their time, it can't be done. They can't run those things around these hills and across these creeks. It just can't be done.'

Well, Sam sent the surveyors to survey the right of way and the old man went down and watched them and he told the surveyors, 'Boys, you're wasting your time. You can't do it.'

Then, the graders came along and he told them the same thing. Well, they finished their grading and laid the cross ties and rails, and my wife and my oldest boys and I were guests of the president of the road and rode over that thirty mile track in his first train.

There was a little station, a little shack built at a place called Nelliesburg."

"Sam invited the countryside to come down and take a ride on the train to the end of the line, free of charge.

Well, on that day, the old-timer was a little late getting down, but he arrived and he walked up to the locomotive and sized it up and down. It was the first time he had seen one, and he said, 'By gum, that's too big. They'll never move her.'

He walked around to the front and walked around on the sidewalk towards the back and about that time Sam told everybody to get on who wanted to get on. He said, 'We're going to take you to the end of the line and bring you back, and it won't cost you anything.' And the old-timer wouldn't get on. Everybody got on but him, and the engineer tooted the whistle and the fireman rang the bell and the train started out slowly, and left the old-timer standing there, straddling the tracks, and it went faster, and faster and faster until it went out of sight. And, the old-timer standing there said, 'By gum, they'll never stop her. They'll never stop her!'" [1]

Captain L.A. Kreimer

The research Joseph Jones did about the Guide Dog Movement paid off in a big way with his selection of the first trainer for International Guiding Eyes.

Lambert Alfred Kreimer was born in Germany in 1893. He was the third generation of his family to serve in the German Forestry Corps, where he began to develop the idea of using dogs to guide the blind.

He was drafted into the German Army in 1911, was wounded in battle seven times, and received his country's highest military honor, the Iron Cross Medal. He was in charge of the German Army's War Dogs Program, teaching dogs to do sentry, messenger and scent work.

Kreimer trained the first dog ever used as a guide for the blind, a small German Shepherd they named "Rolf," to guide a fellow patient at an army field hospital in 1916.

Kaiser Wilhelm II asked Kreimer to become his personal bodyguard, and the young captain guarded the country's leader. The two became friends, and when Kreimer asked to be allowed to return to training dogs, the Kaiser gave him a rare three barrel shotgun as a parting gift and appointed him to run a new program training dogs to lead soldiers that had been blinded in battle.

After the war, Kreimer was appointed head trainer at the large Guide Dog school at Potsdam, where he continued his groundbreaking work.

In 1927, at the request of American John L. Sinykin, Captain Kreimer trained a Shepherd dog named "Lux," and shipped him to the United States to be used as a guide by Senator Thomas D. Schall, of Minnesota, who was visually impaired. President Coolidge, curious upon hearing of a dog being used to guide a member of the Senate, invited Senator Schall and Lux to visit him at the White House.

Kreimer came to the United States in 1929, and worked for Sinykin at his LaSalle Kennels in Minnetonka, Minnesota, teaching German Shepherds to become guide dogs.

He relocated to Burbank, California in 1937, and established his own operation, The Pioneer Training School for Guide Dogs.

Kreimer became a United States citizen on May 9, 1941, and shortly thereafter began working with the United States Army training dogs for the war effort. He was successful in his work with the army and received military honors from the United States Government, the fifth country to so honor him.

He met Joseph W. Jones in 1948, and by the end of that year signed a contract to train dogs exclusively for International Guiding Eyes, which he did until his retirement in 1961.

For the first twelve years of IGE's existence, Kreimer's kennels and home on Virginia Avenue in Burbank served as IGE's training facility and campus, with Kreimer training the dogs and the students, and his wife Fanny doing the cooking and serving as hostess to the students.

Captain L.A. Kreimer died in 1976, at the age of 83. He had trained thousands of dogs, and hundreds of human trainers. His legacy of providing the gift of sight to the visually impaired lives on to this day.

1925.

1924 Staatliche Blindenführerhund Schule. München 192

The german government training school for guide dogs in 1924/1929 in Muenchen, Bayern whit 7 war blind incl. Rudi Jungmeier, Muenchen trained in 1927 whitout arms and his Guide dog Dollie.

Blind Veterans in 1920 from World War # I. in the German
government Training School for Guide Dogs in OLDENBURG.
    The first class trained by X Captain L.A. KREIMER
founder and head of the German Government from 1919 to 1929
          14 blind world war Veterans
           1 blind nurs   and
          15 trainers standind back, also Captain L.A.KREIMER

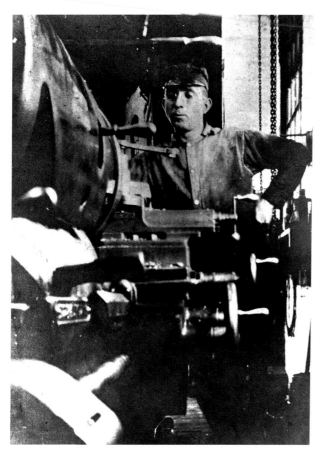

Joseph W. Jones works at his lathe at the New Orleans and Northeastern Railroad shop.

His sight returned gradually, aided by the use of strong eyeglasses, and eight year later, at age sixteen, Joseph Jones followed in his father's footsteps and went to work as a railroad machinist for the New Orleans and Northeastern Railroad. He joined the union at the machine shop, becoming a member of Local Lodge 312 of the International Association of Machinists in 1902. The railroad Jones worked for operated between Meridian and New Orleans, carrying passengers and freight over 196 miles of track. Jones toiled each day over a twenty-four inch motor driven lathe, and according to a speech he delivered some time later, "A number of serious accidents caused me to be blinded two or three times during the time I was working at my trade." [4]

Earl Melton, the man who administered the IAM union oath to Joseph Jones, became his mentor and would eventually become a General Vice Presi-dent of the Machinists Union. Joseph Jones would follow his rise, becoming President of Local Lodge 312, Secretary of the Meridian Central Labor Council, and ultimately Secretary Treasurer of the Mississippi Federation of Labor, a post he would hold for four years. [5]

In 1916, the New Orleans and Northeastern was bought by the Southern Railway. They extended the line north to Cincinnati in what would become known as the "Queen and Crescent Route," a tribute to the nicknames of Cincinnati and New Orleans.

By the early 1920's, Meridian was experiencing remarkable growth. Still the largest city in Mississippi, it was serviced by forty-four trains a day. Mule drawn street cars had given way to electric street cars, and the city's gas lamps had been converted to modern electric street lights. The workforce had grown considerably, and Jones would put in a full day of work at the machine shop and then spend his evenings at the union hall, tending to the needs of his members. He had married and become the father of six children.

All that activity eventually took a toll on Joseph Jones, and his eyesight, always fragile at best, began a rapid deterioration. By 1922, at age thirty-seven, he was no longer able to see well enough to work as a machinist.

According to Jones, "I was compelled to give up my activity in organized labor and the trade. So, I took my family to New York and I went into business to make a living, to finish raising my family of six children. I was fairly successful." [6]

Jones' business in New York, a small lending library, did well for a concern of its size but he later said: "The war came on, and I was compelled to sell out." [7]

With more time on his hands and his vision continuing to deteriorate, Joseph Jones was encouraged by his friends to apply to The Seeing Eye, the school founded by Dorothy Harrison Eustace and Morris Frank, which was then located in New Jersey.

According to Jones: "For a long time, I thought that was a breed of dogs, called '*seeing eye* dogs.'" [8]

"Well, I tried to get one of those dogs," Jones continued, "and I found that it was impossible." [9]

Joseph Jones had been turned down by The Seeing Eye because of his advanced age. He was fifty-seven-years-old.

For a man who had grown up in the rough and tumble labor movement of post-Civil War Meridian, rebounding after meeting with adversity was second nature. Now that he knew what guide dogs were, and how they helped visually impaired people navigate through life, he set out to find out all he could about them.

For the next two years, using his skills as a librarian and the determination that had propelled him upward through the ranks of the labor movement, Joseph Jones conducted a nation-wide survey about guide dogs and guide dogs schools. He spent more than four thousand dollars of his own money in the process.

Jones' survey revealed that there were approximately 225,000 visually impaired people in the United States. He estimated conservatively that if five percent of those people could be given freedom of movement through the use of a guide dog, the need existed for 11,000 guide dogs. The Seeing Eye, located in Morristown, New Jersey, and at the time the nation's largest guide dog school, had only been able to provide 1,400 guide dogs in their twenty years of existence. They also had strict eligibility requirements – such as age – and charged a fee of $150 for their dogs. (Although they waived all fees for war-blinded veterans, and charged only $50 for a second guide dog.)

Jones also found that there were as many as fifty guide dog schools operating in California, but most of them were sham operations set up to collect donations from well meaning benefactors who didn't know that the majority of their gifts were being siphoned off by unscrupulous "trainers."

"I found that the providing of these seeing eye dogs was commercialized or made a racket to a greater of lesser degree," Jones said. "So, I set out to establish an organization that would provide these guide dogs as an outright gift to the blind, because in my survey, I found that the source of supply was limited. The blind people were required to pay or promise to pay, various amounts, when and if they ever got it." [10]

Joseph Jones realized that establishing an organization to provide guide dogs free of charge would be a monumental undertaking.

"It seems like an impossible task that I have undertaken," Jones said, "to provide at least ten thousand blind people with a guide dog that will give them their freedom and independence, release them from the darkness, take them to the places that they want to go. I fully realize the proportions of this undertaking, but none will tell me that it can't be done." [11]   ●

Chapter 3
Guiding Eyes

Joseph Jones established his guide dog organization, which he named Guiding Eyes, on Myrtle Avenue in the Richmond Hill neighborhood of the borough of Queens on Long Island, New York. He filed the necessary paperwork with the State of New York and became a non-profit, non-sectarian corporation in May, 1945.

Located almost exactly at the halfway point between what are now La-Guardia and John F. Kennedy Airports, Richmond Hill was an unlikely place to raise and train guide dogs. Jones realized this and viewed the location as temporary until he could locate and afford to purchase a more suitable site. He soon found a piece of property on the South Shore of Long Island, a place with "buildings and facilities suitable for a school, where the blind may make their temporary home while being instructed in the practical use and handling of a scientifically trained Guide Dog." [1]

Jones knew nothing about training dogs, so he made a deal with a local dog trainer, William P. Holzman, to become Supervisor of Training. Holzman had run his own dog training school in New York for twenty-five years, and had recently been discharged from the U.S. Army, where he had supervised training for the famous K-9 Corps.

Formed by an order from Under Secretary of War Robert P. Patterson in March, 1942, the K-9 Corps was intended to provide dogs for sentry duty, scouting, patrols, delivering messages, and sniffing

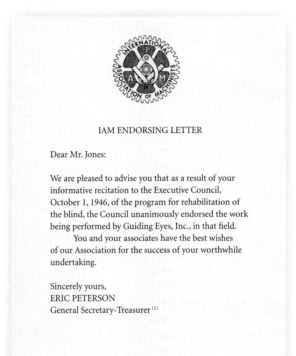

IAM ENDORSING LETTER

Dear Mr. Jones:

We are pleased to advise you that as a result of your informative recitation to the Executive Council, October 1, 1946, of the program for rehabilitation of the blind, the Council unanimously endorsed the work being performed by Guiding Eyes, Inc., in that field.

You and your associates have the best wishes of our Association for the success of your worthwhile undertaking.

Sincerely yours,
ERIC PETERSON
General Secretary-Treasurer [1]

out mines. The government didn't have time during the war to breed their own dogs, so they put out a plea for families to donate "Dogs for Defense," and soon 18,000 canines from thirty-two different breeds descended upon Army training centers. The Army decided that only seven of those breeds met their requirements, and before long nearly 8,000 dogs had been returned to their owners because they were the wrong breed or because of health or behavioral problems. The rest, mostly German Shepherds, Doberman Pinschers and Belgian Sheep Dogs, underwent an eight to twelve week "basic training" to become accustomed to life in the military. [2]

Holzman, like his counterparts at Dorothy Harrison Eustace's Fortunate Fields, had never specifically trained dogs to be guides for the blind, but he had extensive experience working with German Shepherds, the preferred breed for Guide Dogs at the time.

With little in the way of personal financial resources to get things started, Jones turned to his brothers and sisters in the labor movement for help. Earl Melton, the man who had initiated Joseph Jones into the Machinists Union, was now a member of the union's Executive Council, its governing body.

With a little urging from Melton, the Machinists' *Monthly Journal*, an influential publication mailed to the homes of all 600,000 members of the union, ran an article in its May, 1946 edition, explaining the Guiding Eyes program, and soliciting referrals from local lodges across the United States and Canada of "any member, or any other person known to them who is blind and may be interested in securing a Guide Dog." (3)

The article was headlined: "Guiding Eyes, Inc.," and featured the organization's brand new logo, an alert looking German Shepherd, surrounded by a circle containing the words "Our gift to the blind" and "Scientifically trained Guide Dogs." (4)

Jones explained that the purpose of Guiding Eyes was: "To provide a scientifically trained Guide Dog as a gift for every blind person in the United States who desires and who can be aided through one, at the earliest possible date." (5)

Melton also counseled Jones to seek the formal endorsement of the IAM and of his former labor colleagues in Mississippi as a mean s of establishing his legitimacy and generating more contributions.

Jones contacted his old friends in Meridian, and within weeks they responded with an endorsing resolution:

"**Endorsing Resolution**
BE IT RESOLVED, by the Meridian Central Labor Union, that we wholeheartedly endorse GUIDING EYES, INC. and its Founder and President, Joseph W. Jones, Sr., and recommend to any individual or organization interested in aiding the blind, that they too extend to this organization their moral and financial support in this gigantic undertaking to aid the blind of our Nation." (6)

Next, Melton managed to get Jones on the agenda for the fall meeting of the IAM's eleven member Executive Council. White cane in hand, Joseph Jones made his way to the IAM Building in Washington, DC, to make his pitch. On Tuesday, October 1, 1946, a warm overcast day in the nation's capitol, Jones made his presentation to the council. Harvey Brown, the famously gruff and sometimes impatient International President of the Union, listened to Jones' presentation and then began firing questions at him. Wasn't there already an organization in New Jersey that trained Guide Dogs? Who was going to be doing the training?

How much was all of this going to cost?

With the members of the Executive Council looking on, Jones explained calmly that there was indeed an organization already training Guide Dogs, but that they had stringent eligibility guidelines that would prevent many members of the Machinists Union from qualifying, and noted that he, himself, had been turned down for being too old. Training would be handled by William P. Holzman, late of the Army's K-9 Corps. And while it cost about $800 to produce a trained Guide Dog, Jones explained that he wanted to give them to visually impaired people free of charge, since he considered the $150 charge (approximately $1,600 in 2011 money) too burdensome for many people coping with blindness.

Melton looked on with pride as his former protégé won over the skeptical Brown and the rest of the council, and then made a motion that the IAM endorse Guiding Eyes. The motion was adopted unanimously, and General Secretary-Treasurer Eric Patterson was instructed to publish an endorsing letter in an upcoming edition of the Monthly Journal. (7)

Patterson's letter, and a lengthy article explaining the mission of Guiding Eyes and calling for the full support of the Machinists Union, was published in the November issue.

"Just as an example of the possibilities of mass donations," the article said, "the membership of the I.A. of M. could supply a guide dog to every blind person in this country who could use one, by the donation of $10.00 per member. This could be done on the form of a pledge of $.50 per month or more until the total was given. Such a plan could be handled by a special committee in each lodge, and if it were accomplished, every member could look with pride whenever he saw a blind person walking confidently by, guided by man's best friend, a loyal, alert, well-trained and loving dog, a gift from a union with a heart." (8)

Joseph Jones, Sr. and the International Association of Machinists had begun a partnership that would last the rest of his life and beyond.

Guiding Eyes was off and running. (11) ●

Chapter 4
Moving West

The response Joseph Jones got from his pitch to the Machinists Union was swift and substantial. Members from across the United States and Canada who read of the union's endorsement of Guiding Eyes in the November, 1946, *Monthly Journal* began contributing immediately. Some local lodges pledged monthly donations for a fixed period. Others sent monies from their treasuries or from the donations of individual members. IAM District 15 in New York held a benefit variety show and raised nearly four thousand dollars for the cause.

Beginning what would become a tradition, one of the union's General Vice Presidents, Samuel R. Newman, took a seat on the Board of Directors of Guiding Eyes, serving without compensation.

Jones continued to peruse his dream of purchasing a site on the seashore for his school, but was unable to secure enough funds to make it a reality. He did, however, mange to purchase a purebred German Shepherd and to pay William Holzman to train her.

Jones meets with Dorothy Scott, chair of the California Board of Guide Dogs for the Blind. A skeptic at first, Scott would later say that "A larger part of the money donated to International Guiding Eyes goes toward helping the blind than that of any other charitable organization I know of."

That first Guide Dog, named "Young Buche of Groyullam," was given to Arthur Torgerson, of St. Louis, Missouri, in early 1947. [1]

With the new mobility afforded him by use of his guide dog, Torgerson entered the Swedish Institute for Massage in St. Louis, and reported to Jones that things were going so well that he planned to study to be a chiropractor after he received his certificate.

Guiding Eye's next dog was trained for Lloyd Carothers, the thirty-eight-year-old son of an IAM member from Oakland, California. Carothers traveled to New York by plane, and was put up at the Central Queens Y.M.C.A., where Holtzman would collect him each morning for training with his guide dog "Cora." The members IAM Lodge 1566, where Carother's father belonged, were so grateful they voted to contribute twenty-five dollars a month to Guiding Eyes from the union's treasury.

Jones and Holzman would train and deploy a total of eleven more Guide Dogs over the next year. [2]

While he was raising money, screening applicants and trying to find a suitable home for Guiding Eyes, Jones kept up his research about the guide dog movement. One interesting fact he uncovered was that Captain Lambert A. Kreimer, who, as a member of the German Army had been the first man to train a guide dog, and later became the head trainer at Potsdam, had left Germany and immigrated to the United States.

Jones found out that Kreimer was now located in Burbank, California, where he had established "The Pioneer Training School For Guide Dogs" in 1937, the name a proud proclamation of his pioneer work in training guide dogs for the visually impaired.

Jones ventured west to meet with Kreimer and was impressed that Southern California would be a satisfactory place to launch his guide dog school.

The Shrine Auditorium in Hollywood, scene of the Academy Awards, played host to the first International Guiding Eyes fundraiser in California, in June, 1948.

Joseph W. Jones and actress Lynne Roberts present a guide dog to Esther Gray during the benefit show.

The state of California had recently begun licensing guide dog trainers, and Captain Kreimer had been the first person in the state to receive accreditation. The IAM local in the vicinity was District 727, which serviced workers at the Lockheed Aircraft Corporation in Burbank, and it was headed by Ivan Deach, Jr., who was recognized as an innovative and energetic leader. Deach offered Jones the use of free office space at the local's headquarters on Lankershim Boulevard in North Hollywood, and provided clerical staff and moral support for the fledgling effort.

Jones moved his family from New York to the west coast and filed to become a California nonprofit corporation. He soon learned that the name Guiding Eyes, Incorporated, was already taken. In his speech to the 1948 Machinists Grand Lodge Convention, Jones explained: "The reason we adopted the name, 'International Guiding Eyes' is this: We could not file under the laws of California under the name of Guiding Eyes, for the simple reason that Guiding Eyes was not available for us in the state of California. There is an organization, I understand, with a name a little similar. They have no institution. The man is not even licensed, but anyway, we could not use Guiding Eyes in California, so we adopted, International Guiding Eyes, Incorporated." [3]

Jones found the combination of free office space, a better deal with Kreimer than he had with Holzman, and the temperate climate a winning combination. "We have moved to the West Coast," Jones said, "for this reason: We can produce these dogs for at least half of the amount of money that it has been costing us on the East Coast, and we can provide these dogs in Southern California, twelve months in the year, and on the East Coast they can only be trained about nine months in the year." [4]

Another benefit of being located in North Hollywood was its proximity to the galaxy of stars from radio, television and the movies that were plying their trade in the area. District 727's Ivan Deach was able to introduce Jones to some of the leaders of the industry, and thus began a second relationship between International Guiding Eyes and a major source of funding that would last for generations.

Jones (center, with cane) and his son Dick Jones (4th from right) join actors Larry Sims, Penny Singleton, Arthur Lane, Marjorie Kent, and "Daisy the dog," the "Bumstead family" of the movie series "Blondie" at the show.

In June, 1948, eleven IAM local lodges joined forces to sponsor a benefit for International Guiding Eyes at Hollywood's famous Shrine Auditorium, the site of the annual Academy Awards ceremony. Twenty acts from across the entertainment community performed, including Lynne Roberts, an actress from Twentieth Century-Fox who appeared in several movies with the famous cowboy Roy Rodgers (who would also soon become active raising funds for IGE). Columbia Pictures sent the cast from their highly successful movie series "The Bumsteads," featuring Penny Singleton as Blondie and Arthur Lake as Dagwood. Donald O'Connor, a Universal Studios movie star and talented song and dance man, served as the celebrity master of ceremonies. O'Connor was so impressed with the mission of the nascent organization that he became an active supporter and honorary chairman. Jones used the occasion to present a Guide Dog, to Esther Gray, the daughter of an IAM member.

The dog Gray received was one of the first trained for IGE by Captain Kreimer. At the time, Kreimer maintained a string of seven dogs in training but would only accept one human student at a time. He charged IGE a flat fee of four hundred dollars to train each dog and student.

Jones soon entered into an agreement with Captain Kreimer to train dogs and students exclusively for International Guiding Eyes. Kreimer was to select and train "healthy, intelligent female dogs with fully developed brains and bodies and of reliable temperament." [5]

The agreement between Kreimer and IGE compensated for the fact that Jones hadn't been able to establish a suitable campus to train students. According to the pact, Kreimer was to: "Take students into his home and give them his individual training, with both day and night training on the streets."

"The students will be unified with the dog for excellent performance on the streets, in stores, churches, other public buildings and places, all traffic conditions in both city and country, and training for conduct in the house. The student will receive instructions for his or her home, family, as to conduct to the dog. The student will receive instructions and advice on working conditions favorable to the dog as well as proper care of the dog. The students will receive instructions and advice on how to properly conduct himself or herself in public places with the guide dog." [6]

Keenly aware of the value of publicity in raising funds, Jones trumpeted news of his exclusive contract with the world's foremost guide dog trainer to the media. Soon, the *Hollywood Citizen News* ran a story on the arrangement under the headline: "Burbank Man Trains Dogs for Blind under Guiding Eyes Program."

The headline caught the attention of state authorities who were on the lookout for fraudulent guide dog schools set up to raise funds without actually providing dogs. According to Jones, there were approximately fifty such fronts operating in California at the time.

In November, 1948, the California Department of Professional and Vocational Standards, Board of Guide Dogs for the Blind, sent an investigator to North Hollywood to see if International Guiding Eyes was on the up and up. The arrangement he found was unusual in that International Guiding Eyes wasn't training dogs, Captain Kreimer was, and he had a license. IGE was selecting the students and paying Kreimer for his training services. The investigator reported back to his superiors that both Jones and Kreimer appeared to be honest, and that Kreimer's kennels were: "suitable in every respect, ideally located, and efficiently managed." [7]

Dorothy Scott, Chairman of the California Guide Dog Board, and Evelyn Spaulding, General Manager of the Los Angeles Department of Social Services weren't so sure. How could IGE claim to be a guide dog school if it had no licensed trainers of its own and trained no dogs on its own, they questioned.

The investigator also reported that IGE had little or no money in its treasury, was paying Jones twenty-five dollars a week, and had so far received one application and two letters of inquiry from potential guide dog recipients, facts that also raised eyebrows.

The Director of Professional and Vocational Standards, James A. Arnerich, informed Henry Hicker, Executive Secretary of the California Department of Education, that in his opinion IGE fell within the scope of Section 7210 of the California Code, and thus required a license. Hicker then contacted Ivan Deach, who had assumed the role of General Secretary Treasurer of IGE, and asked that he submit an application.

Jones and Deach filled out the necessary paperwork and applied to the state for a license "to finance the giving of guide dogs." That description of their purpose threw the bureaucracy for a loop. Hicker responded that he would have to ask the Board of Guide Dogs if he could recognize their application, since it wasn't for the traditional request "to conduct a Guide Dog School." He also suggested to Dorothy Scott, Chair of the Board, that she solicit an opinion from the Attorney General to determine if IGE could be given a California license.

The confusion about what to do was best described by Arnerich in a letter to Scott outlining the terms of the question to be posed to the Attorney General:

"It is my opinion that technically the International Guiding Eyes are not in violation of the act if they give dogs to blind people. However, I do not believe that they could be considered in the business of running a school. You will recall that at the last meeting I brought up the problem of service clubs and charitable organizations that raise funds for the purpose of securing guide dogs for some needy person. The operation of International Guiding Eyes, Incorporated, appears to be the same as that of an organization such as the Lions Club, and I do not believe restrictions should be placed on those who are carrying out such a program.

The primary objective is to protect the person who obtains the dog, and if the dog comes from a licensed school this matter is safeguarded. Of course there is the incidental problem of fraudulent solicitation, but as mentioned at several of the meetings, this is a matter that goes beyond the regulation of guide dog schools, and I do not think an attempt should be made to regulate solicitation." [8]

Dorothy Scott turned to the Attorney General for guidance. In a letter dated April 8, 1949, Assistant Attorney General Kenneth Lynch informed Scott that: "It is the opinion of this office that the International Guiding Eyes, Inc., is operating within the law, providing a license is or has been issued to said organization." [9]

Lynch also opined that: "It not only appears that International Guiding Eyes, Inc., is privileged to be licensed (providing they comply with all of the rules and regulations) but also that such an organization would be committing a misdemeanor if it carried out any of said activities without obtaining a license." [10]

Dorothy Scott accepted the opinion of the Attorney General, and made arrangements to visit International Guiding Eyes to inspect the premises and take stock of Joseph W. Jones, Sr.

In her report back to the full board, Scott made it clear she was quite skeptical about Jones and IGE. "The Committee was not favorably impressed by the interview," she wrote, "and it is reluctant to extend the scope of the Act by licensing an organization that does not have its own training facilities but which limits its activities to fundraising 'to finance the giving of guide dogs.'" [11]

Scott must have caught Joseph Jones at an unusual moment, because the usually unflappable founder of IGE is recorded as being almost out of funds and doubtful that any significant income was on the horizon. Instead, it was the typically more taciturn Captain Kreimer who was bubbling with optimism that the funds would roll in and that IGE would one day build its own training facility.

Scott concluded her report to the board: "In view of the wording of the Act and the opinion of the Attorney General's Office, there seems to be no sound reason for rejecting the application. The Committee therefore recommends that the license be issued, but feels that the activities of the organization should be closely observed. [12]

On May 5, 1949, the state of California issued a license to International Guiding Eyes, Incorporated. Within months, Joseph Jones, Captain L.A. Kreimer and the people of IGE, with help from the IAM and the Hollywood community, would turn Dorothy Scott from a skeptic to a true believer in International Guiding Eyes. ●

Chapter 5
The Dream Becomes a Reality

The house in the background, residence of Captain L.A. Kreimer and his wife Fanny, served as school, kennel and student dormitory for the first eleven years of International Guiding Eyes' operations.

With a license from the state in hand and an exclusive contract with the world's foremost guide dog trainer, Joe Jones began a whirlwind of activity that would turn his dream of providing guide dogs to the blind free of charge into a reality. He used a white cane to find his way to the Machinists' office on Lankershim Boulevard in North Hollywood every day where he worked the telephones, dictated correspondence and reviewed applications from prospective students. Meanwhile, Captain L.A. Kreimer was working with dogs and an increasing number of students at his facility on South Virginia Avenue in Burbank, about four miles away. The results were amazing.

Jones was a mastermind at fundraising and publicity. In addition to the substantial financial support he was receiving from an ever expanding fundraising network from the Machinists, he enlisted Hollywood to aid his cause.

MGM Studios donated a collie dog that was an offspring of "Pal," the remarkably talented male collie who played "Lassie" in the 1943 movie "*Lassie Come Home*," and subsequent films. Kreimer trained the collie to be a Guide Dog, and Jones presented her to Nan Farquhar, the daughter of an IAM member from Winnipeg, Canada.

Jones orchestrated an appearance on the popular NBC Radio show, "*Truth or Consequences*," for a prospective student who performed a skit with movie star John Wayne, and was rewarded by host Ralph Edwards informing her that as her prize for participating, she would be enrolled at International Guiding Eyes. Several weeks later, two blind girls sponsored by Los Angeles area chapters of the IAM Women's Auxiliary appeared on Mutual Broadcasting's "*Queen For A Day*," where they told the listening audience that any prizes they received would be donated to International Guiding Eyes. [1]

The effective publicity led to an onslaught of applications from prospective students and offers from hundreds of people who wished to donate dogs for training. Speaking some time later, Jones described the hectic early days at International Guiding Eyes: "The people are very good in this section of Los Angeles," Jones recalled. "They phone in and offer us these

IGE trained only German Shepherds in its early years.

Jones was moved by this scout's request for help.

May Peake (center), International President of the IAM Women's Auxiliary, was an ardent supporter of IGE.

dogs. We do not take them until they are at least eleven months of age so that we are saved the expense of raising them from puppies, and too, if we did attempt to raise them, you might find a whole litter of puppies and not one of them could qualify as a guide dog."

Jones then elaborated on the process he and Kreimer employed in selecting dogs for training: "I have a set of questions I ask them to see if the dog can qualify, and one of the questions is: Did you raise the dog?"

"We will not take a dog from a kennel," Jones continued. "It must be raised in a home where there is at least one child, preferably two."

"We use the female German Shepherd exclusively for the reason that our trainer over his many years of experience has decided that they are the best all-round breed for our purpose."

"If the questions are satisfactorily answered, then I send out our trainer to see the dog. He doesn't miss very often, but we are only able to accept about two out of ten of the dogs that are offered." [2]

Jones then described the screening process Kreimer employed for dogs that passed the first hurdle: "He takes them over to the school, and he puts them through a very rigid test. Then if he is satisfied he takes them another month before he is thoroughly satisfied that the dog will qualify to guide a blind person.

Then when he is satisfied, we send them over to the veterinarian and when they come back, it takes two to three months more to complete that training of that dog to guide a blind person." [3]

Using that rigorous screening and training regi-

men, Jones and Kreimer started to churn out a steady flow of teams of students and guide dogs. Jones held fast to his pledge that no one would be denied a guide dog because of age. "We have provided people with guide dogs," Jones said, "who had reached the age of seventy-one or seventy-two. They were physically fit and alert and we have prolonged the life of many blind people." [4]

Jones related the remarkable stories of two of the students International Guiding Eyes served in their early years:

"There is a case that has touched me more than any other," Jones said. "A Boy Scout phoned me from Southgate, California, and he said he was inquiring as to what they could do to get a guide dog for a member of their troop. He was seventeen years of age. He said, 'What is it going to cost us, Mr. Jones?'"

"I told him that the dog would not cost him anything and I explained how it was made possible through the contributions from lodges, members, and friends of the I.A. of M. and their Ladies Auxiliary. The Boy Scout could hardly understand that. I told him to bring the boy to the office so that we could interview him and have the trainer take him out."

"They brought the boy over and the Boy Scout that phoned me came along, as well as the boy's mother and father. As I sat at my desk talking to this blind boy, the newspaper took a picture of me talking to the boy, and the mother and father said, 'We didn't realize that there was such an organization in existence.'" [5]

Jones' explained that his pride in helping the young man from the scout troop was increased tremendously when the scout master explained that there were twenty-three boys in the troop, and each had a physical handicap. The Boy Scout who phoned him to help his fellow scout had an artificial leg and told the scout master that he was grateful that the new guide dog would do for his friend what his prosthesis did for him: help him navigate his way through the world.

A story Jones related about a man from Fort Worth, Texas was equally compelling. While touring Texas to raise fund for IGE, Jones was approached by staff from a local charity who asked for his help.

"The head of Lighthouse for the Blind called me," Jones recalled, "and said, 'Mr. Jones, we have a young man here and we have done all we can to rehabilitate him. In addition to being totally blind, he is paralyzed in both hands, from the wrists down. We have taught him how to make doormats out of old automobile tires but he cannot sell them because he has nobody to go with him from store to store or door to door. Can you give this man a dog?'"

"At that time I was not sure we could train a person that was paralyzed in both hands and so I called in our trainer and talked to him about it and he said we could. He told me that he had trained them when they didn't have any hands, when they had only hooks for hands.

We brought that man to California and provided him with a guide dog that was trained to work close to his knee, because, having no feeling in his hands, he couldn't tell the movements of the dog through the harness. Therefore, the dog was trained to work close to the man's knee.

This man, although he was totally blind and paralyzed in his hands, was so determined to make a go of it that he learned to read Braille with his tongue and lips – the only blind person I have ever known that could read Braille with his tongue and lips.

When the trainer brought him over to the office, I asked him: 'Bert, do you feel perfectly safe now to go anywhere in the world with the guide dog?' He said: 'Mr. Jones, I feel safe to go anywhere in the world with this guide dog.'" [6]

One problem Jones foresaw was that the man would be unable to put the harness on the dog. Bert assured him that he had a plan, and that he had a good neighbor who would help him.

"A few weeks later I received a letter written in Bert's name," Jones said. "It said: "Mr. Jones, I have a surprise – I can harness my dog; for with the help of my tongue and lips I can put it on." [7]

Applications continued to pour in from across the United States and Canada, and the number of guide dog teams began to increase. Dorothy Scott, the President of the California State Board of Guide Dogs for the Blind, who had been very skeptical when

Peter Gallegos, a member of the Sioux Tribe, and his guide dog "Bonnie," and Johnnie Gordon and his guide "Elizabeth" at an early graduation.

Before it began a breeding program, IGE relied on donated puppies. They preferred puppies raised in households with children.

A Truly International Organization

In the Spring of 1951, Joseph Jones received a telephone call from a young woman who was a student at the Perkins School for the Blind, in Watertown, Massachusetts. Her name was Gloria Cruz, and she was a resident of Manila, Philippines, who had been blind since age six.

Gloria graduated at the top of her high school class in Manila and was awarded a Fulbright Scholarship. After college she spent a year at Perkins training to become a teacher for what, at the time, were called "deaf, dumb and blind" students.

While she was at Perkins, Gloria learned about guide dogs and desperately wanted one. She applied at the East Coast schools and was turned down because they didn't train foreign students. She had heard that International Guiding Eyes was far more inclusive, so she called Jones to inquire about enrolling there.

Jones was receptive to the idea, but the mandatory six months quarantine of any animal entering the Philippines was a real hurdle. Joe Jones called on the IAM for help circumventing the quarantine, and IAM Headquarters leapt into action, deploying their lawyers and lobbyists to Capitol Hill and Embassy Row to straighten things out. After considerable work on their part, the quarantine was waived.

Gloria Cruz traveled to L.A. Kreimer's training facility in Burbank, where Joe Jones greeted her with news that the Sherman Oaks Junior Women's Club had raised the $500 it would take to buy and train her new guide dog.

Never one to pass up an opportunity for publicity, Jones reached out to the United States Information Agency, and their Asian focused publication *Free World* sent a reporter and photographer to capture Gloria training with her new partner, "Anna."

On graduation day, Sofronio Abrera, the Philippine Consul General was on hand to congratulate Gloria Cruz and their photograph was published in a number of newspapers.

Free World published a glowing article about International Guiding Eyes, and soon Joe Jones was fielding phone calls from people in India, Pakistan and throughout Asia, asking for guide dogs.

All of the publicity, training, legal and political wrangling it took to get Gloria and "Anna" back to the Philippines without a quarantine almost was for naught. Gloria and "Anna" departed Los Angeles by ship in August, 1951, to begin their new life together in Manila. Two days after leaving port, Gloria was walking "Anna" on deck and stopped to talk with someone. "Anna" panicked at the movement of the ship and jumped overboard. Gloria was horrified. The captain of the ship learned of the tragedy and immediately brought the ship about to rescue the dog. He stopped the ship, lowered a lifeboat and sent four of his best sailors to retrieve poor "Anna." They returned to the ship with a very wet, very scared guide dog, who lived to become the first American trained guide dog in the Philippines.

IGE was issued a license, returned for another inspection in mid-1950, and was so impressed with the progress that Jones and Kreimer had made that she told the press, "A larger part of the money donated to International Guiding Eyes goes toward helping the blind than that of any other charitable organization I know of." [8]

They churned out eighteen guide dog teams the first year, with students staying at Kreimer's house on South Virginia Avenue in Burbank, and Jones manning the office at the IAM local on Lankershim Boulevard in North Hollywood.

Jones, still aided only by his white cane, traveled extensively to promote IGE and to raise funds. He made appearances in Fort Worth, and Port Arthur, Texas, Carlsbad, New Mexico, and dozens of other cities. He spoke to union meetings, boy scout and girl scout troops, local chambers of commerce and just about any group he could corral long enough to make his pitch.

He used his ready access to the local newspapers and the nationally circulated Machinists *Monthly Journal* and weekly newspaper to entice politicians, business leaders, union officials and movie stars to award certificates to IGE graduates, promising them a flattering picture, suitable for framing.

By year three, the number of teams trained had reached 83, with a steady flow of new students keeping the beds at Kreimer's house occupied.

In 1952, Jones traveled to Kansas City, Missouri to address the quadrennial Grand Lodge Convention of the IAM. He tapped his way to the podium with his white cane and proudly reported to the assembled delegates that International Guiding Eyes, Incorporated, was now a going concern, thanks to their help and support. He talked about the process they employed for se-

The guide dog harness was invented by Captain L.A. Kreimer, the first trainer for International Guiding Eyes.

lecting, training and deploying guide dogs, and related the stories of several graduates. He noted with pride that the vast majority of the members of his board of directors were officers of the Machinists Union, and referred to the detailed financial report provided to each delegate.

Jones closed his remarks with a touching reflection on his own circumstances. "I sincerely prayed to God for two things," Jones said. "After my wife passed away and left me with a ten year old boy, I prayed that I would be spared long enough to see this organization well established and that my ten year old boy would become a man. Both prayers have been answered. The organization is well established, it is in the hands of the International Association of Machinists and my boy is a man, and I am proud to say that today he is a member of the International Association of Machinists." [9]

The delegates were so moved by Jones' presentation that they took up not one, but two, collections. The first, for IGE, raised several thousand dollars. Then, noting that Jones himself was without the aid of a guide dog despite all he had done to found the organization and help dozens of other visually impaired people, the delegates reached into their pockets a second time and took up a collection earmarked for a specific project. A thousand one dollar bills from IAM delegates bought a lovely German Shepherd named Lucy Belle and provided the funds to train her and Joseph Walter Jones, Sr., their brother and the founder of IGE.

Jones' prayer for a successful organization had been answered and now, ten years after he was rejected for being too old, his dream of having a guide dog partner would finally be realized.   ●

Chapter 6
Transitions

Joe Jones and Lucy Belle, whom he usually just called "Lucy," did a wonderful job representing International Guiding Eyes. They became a familiar sight at IAM events across the country as Jones continued to ask for support, and IAM members continued to give their time, money and muscle to grow the organization.

Jones and his trainer, Captain L. A. Kreimer, were both in their seventies and despite the incredible drive that had allowed each of them to be pioneers in their field, they realized they needed to bring along the next generation to sustain what they had built.

Jones turned A. D. "Duke" Evers, a young business agent from IAM, Local Lodge 727, where he maintained the office of International Guiding Eyes, and appointed him General Manager. Evers would handle the day to day operations of IGE, and Jones would spend more time as roving ambassador, generating publicity and raising funds.

Captain Kreimer, who had trained thousands of dogs, and hundreds of trainers, chose a young protégé named Erich Renner to be his Assistant Trainer, with an eye toward his taking the reigns when the time came for him to retire.

Jones also kept a steady stream of Hollywood celebrities, local political dignitaries and representatives of various service clubs coming to IGE graduation events. Each new team of student and guide dog offered an opportunity for publicity, and Joe Jones made the most of it.

One thing that concerned Jones greatly was that IGE had not yet purchased a permanent home. The IGE administrative offices, which had been located for many years at IAM Lodge 727 on Lankershim Boulevard in North Hollywood, moved to more spacious quarters on Collins Street, but dogs and students were still housed at Captain Kreimer's residence on Virginia Street in Burbank.

Members of the Firefighter's Union from Burbank, California, joined many other labor organizations in supporting the work of IGE.

Joseph W. Jones, Sr., addresses the 1956 IAM Convention in San Francisco, with his guide dog Lucy Belle at his side. Jones waited ten years from founding IGE before taking a guide dog for himself.

IAM President Al Hayes, who led his union's efforts to aid IGE, experiences the sensation of being led by "Lucy," Joseph W. Jones' guide dog.

In the spring of 1956, the IGE Board of Directors voted to purchase a piece of land on Denny Avenue, North Hollywood, about four miles from Captain Kreimer's facility. With a little prodding from Joe Jones, the Architect's Association of San Fernando Valley contributed a complete set of blueprints and specifications for what would soon become IGE's first permanent home.

That September, Joe Jones and his faithful guide "Lucy" made their way to San Francisco to address the 1956 IAM Grand Lodge Convention. As he had done at past conventions, Jones thanked the delegates for their generous support and recounted the stories of several students who had received guide dogs from IGE.

He reported proudly that there were now 195 graduates of IGE, and that more students and dogs were being trained each month.

In a moment of unusual candor, he confessed: "I become discouraged at times. It gets monotonous looking into darkness eternally. But, something happens almost every day to make me get down on my knees and thank Almighty God for the many blessings he had bestowed on me and mine." [1]

"It has been my desire from the beginning," Jones said, "to make International Guiding Eyes, Incorporated, a credit to the International Association of Machinists. I am proud of our standing locally, in the state, and nationally." [2]

Nine months after that convention speech, before ground was broken for the new IGE training facility, Joseph W. Jones, Sr. succumbed to a heart attack at the age of 72. He was survived by five children and eleven grand children.   ●

Captain L.A. Kreimer, IGE's first trainer, chose fellow German immigrant Erich Renner to succeed him.

tain L. . Kreimer, Daniel C. Hart and GUIDE DOG "Ginger", and
sistant Trainer, Erich Renner.

Early graduation ceremonies were held at the Kreimer residence on South Virginia Avenue in Burbank.

After some initial objections, airlines began accommodating guide dogs in the early 1950's.

IAM Vice President Roy Brown presents graduates with their certificates in 1951.

Actress Lillian Randolph, who starred as "Beulah" on television, congratulates two graduates.

Joseph Lamphier, who would eventually serve a brief term as President of IGE, presents a guide dog to James D.
Alexander of St. James, Winnipeg, Canada.

IGE graduated an almost equal number of men and women.

S.G. "Goodie" Goodman (left) would serve a brief term as President of IGE after founder Joseph W. Jones, Sr. passed away. The position of President became mostly ceremonial until 1973.

This 1951 graduation ceremony took place in the living room of the Kreimer residence.
Students stayed there during their training period and Mrs. Kreimer served as cook and den mother.

Joseph W. Jones traveled extensively throughout the US and Canada to promote IGE and raise funds.

Every IGE graduation ceremony provided a photo opportunity for political figures and philanthropists.
The man on the right was a Vice President of Lockheed Aircraft Company.

Joe Jones had moved to California in 1948, but seven years later, in 1955, he still subscribed to the Long Island Press. A story he read in that newspaper in September of that year tugged at his heartstrings, and he decided to do something about it.

The story concerned the miraculous recovery of three-year-old Rosemary Marazzo of Long Island City, New York. Rosemary had fallen out of a fifth floor window of her parent's apartment and survived. The story related how she had been sorely missed during her convalescence at St. John's hospital, not only because her parents loved her, but also because she served as the "eyes" for her thirty-year-old mother, Victoria, who was totally blind. Young Rosemary would lead her mother to the grocery store and any other necessary errands, and she also helped her care for her infant brother, Victor. Rosemary's father, Frank, was also partially blind, and he worked in the laundry at Mary Immaculate Hospital, making a minimal living.

Jones was so touched by the Marazzo's fate that he contacted a business agent at IAM District 15 in New York and asked him to approach the Marazzo's with an offer of help. He did so, and District 15 paid the airfare to fly Victoria Marazzo to California where IGE provided her with a guide dog and four weeks of training.

With the help of Joe Jones, the IAM and the training staff at IGE the quality of life for the Marazzo family improved dramatically.

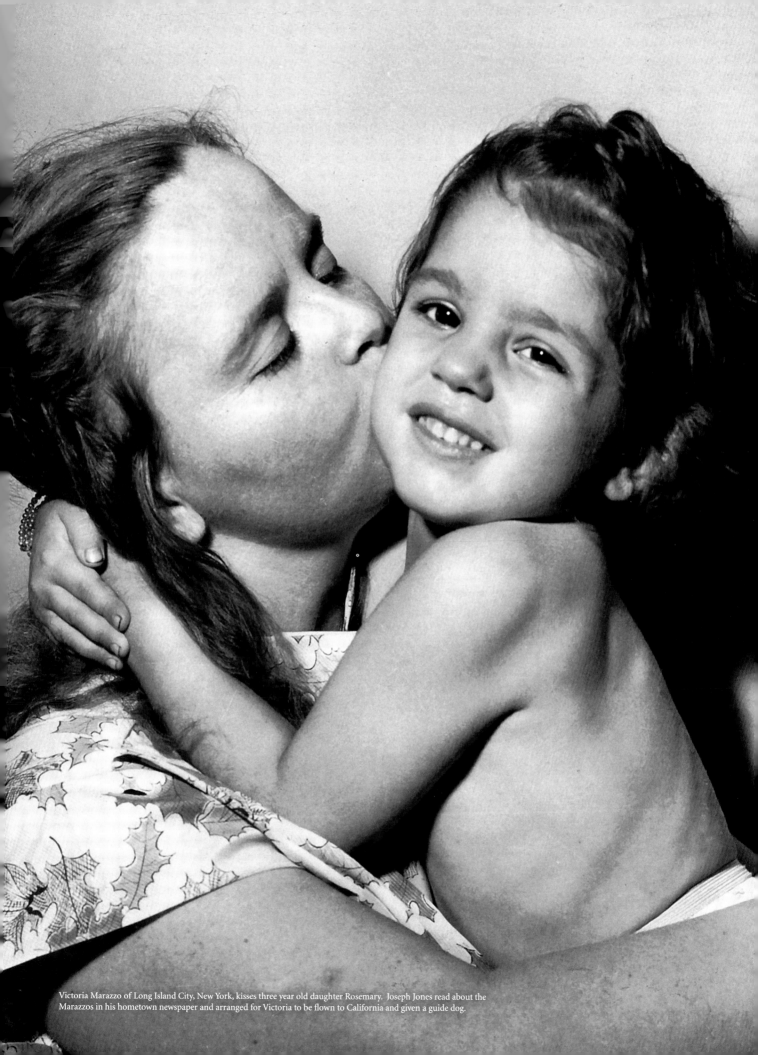

Victoria Marazzo of Long Island City, New York, kisses three year old daughter Rosemary. Joseph Jones read about the Marazzos in his hometown newspaper and arranged for Victoria to be flown to California and given a guide dog.

Many IAM local lodges formed shop committees to raise funds for International Guiding Eyes.

Chapter 7
A New Home

The International Guiding Eyes Board of Directors met the day after funeral services for founder Joseph Jones, and decided that Duke Evers would continue to run the day to day operations at IGE. They also voted to make the position of President largely ceremonial with a one year term. Herbert A. Cooksey, the fifty-one-year-old President of District Lodge 94 of the IAM, was elected.

The President and board members were all connected to the IAM in one way or another and served IGE without pay. John Snider, the President of District 727 and Secretary Treasurer of IGE, convinced IAM headquarters to allow him to "lend" Duke Evers to IGE while keeping him on the IAM payroll.

The board of directors was determined to see Joe Jones' legacy live on in the form of a successful organization, and voted to move forward with plans to build their own facility. Two years later, after a massive fundraising effort, they broke ground on Denny Avenue, in North Hollywood, where a sparkling new facility would soon take shape.

On March 3, 1960, they dedicated the new building, which for the first time allowed International Guiding Eyes, Incorporated, to house their administrative offices, kennel, training quarters for students, and a residence for their head trainer, all in one place.

Built at a cost of $45,000, the new facility boasted dormitory rooms for up to ten students, bunked two to a room, "with a radio in each room," a "spacious dining room lounge," and an "all electric kitchen, where Mrs. Erich Renner prepares tasty, nourishing food for our students." [1]   The kennel area featured runs for ten dogs, and the administrative offices were equipped with brand new desks and chairs.

The IAM continued to raise money for IGE, including a program run by the Ladies Auxiliary selling dinner baskets at Easter, Thanksgiving and Christmas, with the proceeds going to help keep the school running.

Duke Evers followed Joe Jones' tradition of bringing celebrities and Hollywood stars to IGE, and named movie star Donald O'Connor, who had performed at the very first IGE benefit in 1948, as Honorary Chair of the organization.

On February 1, 1960, the "*DuPont Show, starring June Allyson,*" aired an episode filmed at IGE, called "So Dim The Light," featuring Allyson as an actress who had lost her sight but regained her dignity and mobility with the help of a friendly trainer, played by actor Robert Culp, and a noble guide dog, played by a German Shepherd trained at IGE.

Former California Governor Goodwin Knight and his wife Virginia presided over one of the first graduation ceremonies at the Denny Avenue facility, and they were followed by such luminaries as Jackie Cooper, Roy Rogers, Zsa Zsa Gabor and Lucille Ball. [2]

Through the next decade, International Guiding Eyes, Incorporated continued to grow and prosper. IAM Grand Lodge Representative John Foote took over as President in 1964, Joseph D. Lamphier, a Business Representative from local lodge 727 took over in 1965, S.G. "Goodie" Goodman, the Financial Secretary of local lodge 311 in Los Angeles became President in 1968, and Irvin P. Mazzci, a onetime entertainer who was President of the Los Angeles County Federation of Labor, became President in 1969.

Erich Renner, the German-born protégé of Captain Kreimer remained as head trainer, with his wife serving as cook and unofficial den mother, until 1965. When Renner left IGE, he was followed by Lee Muehlenberg, described by newspapers as "a good looking woman, about 30," who served for three years, and Arthur Marinaccio, who served for two years and brought his son, Arthur Marinaccio, Jr., along as an

Herbert A. Cooksey (center) was the first to serve in the ceremonial post of IGE President after founder Joseph W. Jones, Sr. passed away.

assistant trainer. [3] While Muehlenberg and Marinaccio were competent and licensed by the state of California, they lacked the charisma of Kreimer and Renner. In 1970, the IGE board convinced Renner to return to the school and revamp the training program.

The IAM were able to convince their brothers and sisters in the labor movement of the value of International Guiding Eyes, and when the Denny Avenue facility needed a coat of paint, Local 1595 of the International Association of Painters and Allied Trades were on hand with rollers and brushes to accomplish the job. When the kennel runs started to show the effects of generations of guide dogs sharpening their teeth on the wooden frames, Carpenter's Local 1913 showed up with hammers and saws and refurbished it to like new condition. [4]

Donald O'Connor continued to support IGE as he had since its earliest days in California, and brought a steady stream of fellow stars to fundraising events and graduations. In 1970, at O'Connor's urging, Andy Griffith, of the popular television show *"The Andy Griffith Show,"* became the first Hollywood star to donate the entire cost of training a guide dog, $3,500 at the time, so that Bobby Fierce of Overland, Missouri could be paired with guide dog "Georgia," his new source of independence. [5]

A decade after his passing, the organization that Joseph Jones, Sr. had conceived because he was denied a guide dog had made the transition from a small group centered on his own drive and personality to a full-fledged international organization that chose the motto: *"We Serve...That Others May See."*   ●

C. C. Bogardus, Al Smith, Wm. E. Burk, Kenneth Sharp, Lloyd Poesnecker, John Foote, Murial Stamm, Secy. to the Board, Anthony Ballerini, H. A. Cooksey, S. G. Goodman, John Snider, Genevieve Anderson, Al Klein, Mrs. Verne Trotta, E. H. Vernon
Front row - A. D. Evers, Harry A. Baele
6-6-57

Irvin P. Mazzci (center) served a brief term as IGE President in 1969.

James B. Garfield and GUIDE DOG "Fiera" in front of station wagon. Mr. Garfield graduated April 15, 1960, and is president of California State Board of Guide Dogs for the Blind. Kennels are shown in the background.

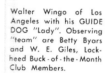

John J. Hess, Jr., St. Louis, Mo. and GUIDE DOG "Lady" with June Allyson, TV, Movie Star.

Walter Wingo of Los Angeles with his GUIDE DOG "Lady". Observing "team" are Betty Byars and W. E. Giles, Lockheed Buck-of-the-Month Club Members.

Students Wm. Stuessel, Glendale; Sam Schechter, Los Angeles; Maurice M. Craft, Inglewood; James B. Garfield, Los Angeles with their GUIDE DOGS on Graduation Day April 15, 1960, with A. D. Evers, Erich Renner, Robert Culp, Mrs. Culp and TV Commentators & Radio Stations represented. Friends and relatives of students are also pictured.

International Guiding Eyes, inc.

"We Serve that Others Might See"

Sponsored By The

INTERNATIONAL ASSOCIATION of MACHINISTS
AFL-CIO
"The Union With a Heart"

Step 1
Trainer instructs student in proper use of harness.

Step 2
New student is introduced to his Guide Dog.

Step 3
Students learn to work with their Guide Dogs in Obedience Training.

Step 4
Cautiously guides master around danger.

Guide Dogs in Action

Step 5
Alertly observes traffic and guides master safely across busy intersection.

Step 6
Climbing steps safely.

Step 7
Descending steps safely.

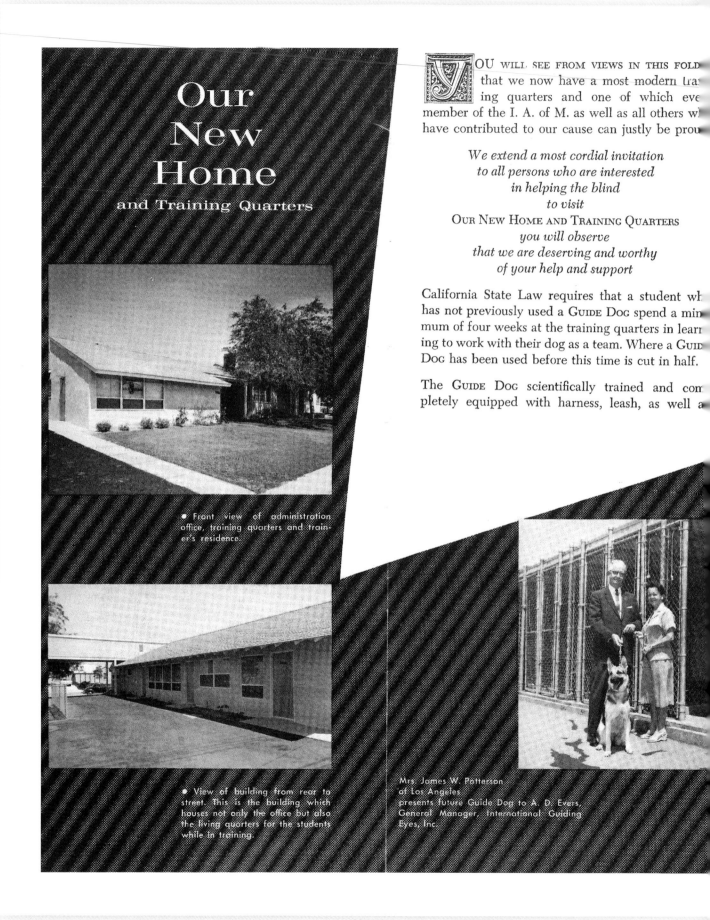

Our New Home
and Training Quarters

● Front view of administration office, training quarters and trainer's residence.

● View of building from rear to street. This is the building which houses not only the office but also the living quarters for the students while in training.

YOU WILL SEE FROM VIEWS IN THIS FOLD that we now have a most modern training quarters and one of which every member of the I. A. of M. as well as all others who have contributed to our cause can justly be proud.

*We extend a most cordial invitation
to all persons who are interested
in helping the blind
to visit*
OUR NEW HOME AND TRAINING QUARTERS
*you will observe
that we are deserving and worthy
of your help and support*

California State Law requires that a student who has not previously used a GUIDE DOG spend a minimum of four weeks at the training quarters in learning to work with their dog as a team. Where a GUIDE DOG has been used before this time is cut in half.

The GUIDE DOG scientifically trained and completely equipped with harness, leash, as well a

Mrs. James W. Patterson of Los Angeles presents future Guide Dog to A. D. Evers, General Manager, International Guiding Eyes, Inc.

eing inoculated, is presented to the person as an outright gift. In addition to this the student receives board and lodging, at no cost, while attending our training school.

Of course, it is easy to understand that this all costs money and now that we have increased our facilities it will cost even more. We are, therefore, appealing to you for increased donations to enable us to continue our work in helping the blind by providing them with properly trained GUIDE DOGS. If you know a worthy person 16 years of age or over who needs and can use a GUIDE DOG, please write us and we will gladly send application forms either to you or the sightless person.

Any person, club, or organization may sponsor one of these GUIDE DOGS, or may help to provide one by making a voluntary contribution in any amount.

We employ no paid promoters, solicitors or fund raising organizations.

Every cent goes for providing GUIDING EYE DOGS for the blind.

Please mail your contribution today . . . an attractive SPONSOR'S CARD will be immediately sent to you, identifying you as a donor to this worthy, humanitarian cause.

All contributions are tax exempt.

Students find fellowship and recreation in spacious dining-room lounge.

Mrs. Erich Renner at oven in our all electric kitchen where wholesome, tasty, nourishing food is prepared for our students.

Kurt Herrmann, kennel master in front of kennels.

Dormitory. Students and their GUIDE DOGS share this room which has beds for two as well as twin wardrobes. There is a radio in each room.

Our organization is supported ENTIRELY *by voluntary contributions, a large portion of which comes from lodges, members, and friends of the International Association of Machinists and their Ladies' Auxiliaries. In addition, other groups as well as religious, service, civic and fraternal organizations and individuals, like yourself, in all walks of life voluntarily contribute to this humanitarian program*

NOEL COALSON
AND HIS GUIDE DOG
"DUTCHESS)

GUIDE DOG 'GEORGIA

The Kohler family welcomes a new addition, guide dog "Herman," who would give 29-year-old Mrs. Ada Kohler newfound mobility.

A.D. "Duke" Evers, (left) IGE General Manager, presides over a graduation in 1959. Joseph Jones chose Evers to lead the day to day functions of IGE, and once Jones passed away, Evers ran the school while the President's post became largely ceremonial.

Learning How to Avoid Hazards

Finding telephone booth

Since Guide Dogs must have the ability to learn and retain a number of special services, we select dogs for quality and a high degree of intelligence.

During a four months training period our dogs must learn the qualities of observation, patience, faithful watchfulness and to a certain degree, the exercise of judgment.

After our licensed trainer has taught our dogs to work as leaders of the blind they are individually matched to a sightless master.

Walking down steps

Avoiding concrete bench

Shopping with Master

Guidance toward a waiting bus

Waiting for the "go" sign

Crosswalk means safety

Lodge 1857,(B.C. Auto Workers) of Vancouver, B.C., Canada, remembering the motto "The Union with a heart" sponsored Mr. Anthony Affleck of Keremeos, B.C., Canada, in the acquisition of a Seeing Eye dog.

Working in conjunction with the Canadian National Institute for the Blind, Lodge 1857 selected Mr. Affleck and sent him for training to the Guiding Eyes establishment at Burbank, California.

G.L.R. Jim McMillan and Officials of Lodge 1857 were on hand to welcome Mr. Afflect on his return to Vancouver and the praise he bestowed on the Guiding Eyes organization was well founded on seeing the wonderful under-standing that already existed between Tony Affleck and his dog "Janie".

Actor Donald O'Connor (center) served as celebrity emcee at the 1948 benefit and became Honorary Chairman of IGE.
He donated a significant amount of his own money to IGE and convinced many fellow Hollywood stars to support the school.

Heidi Banks

Audrey Whetzel graduated from International Guiding Eyes in April, 1964, and was partnered with "Heidi," an attractive black female German Shepherd.

Audrey and "Heidi" went to work for IGE, traveling around the country speaking at conventions and appearing before service groups to put a human (and canine) face on IGE's fundraising efforts.

The pair proved to be a popular draw, and Whetzel penned a poem to her partner that was widely circulated:

Heidi

Tho not a word can Heidi say
She lets me know in every way –
By my side she'll always be,
Watching, loving, guiding me.

Her warm, wet tongue upon my cheek,
Her quick response each time I speak –
Oh how I thank the Lord above
For sending Heidi me to love

Ready now to take my place among society,
The chains of blindness gone for good,
My Heidi set me free.

How bright Life is with Heidi near,
This darkness I'll no longer fear,
She'll take me where I want to go –
Heidi, how I love you so,
Heidi, how I love you so."

In 1968, "Heidi" was immortalized in ceramic and placed atop small wooden collection boxes dubbed "Heidi Banks." The boxes were made for IGE free of charge by boys in the Ontario, California youth detention facility. [1]

Heidi Banks soon started appearing at grocery store and on the counters of convenience stores across the state where customers were encouraged to donate spare change to help finance International Guiding Eyes, Incorporated.

Audrey Whetzel and "Heidi."

Heidi banks were displayed on checkout counters throughout Southern California to collect spare change for IGE.

Heidi

Tho not a word can Heidi say
She lets me know in every way —
By my side she'll always be,
Watching, loving, guiding me.

Her warm, wet tongue upon my cheek,
Her quick response each time I speak —
Oh how I thank the Lord above
For sending Heidi me to love.

Ready now to take my place among society,
The chains of blindness gone for good,
My Heidi set me free.

How bright Life is with Heidi near,
This darkness I'll no longer fear,
She'll take me where I want to go —
Heidi, how I love you so,
Heidi, how I love you so.

Chapter 8
Growing Pains

By the early 1970's, International Guiding Eyes was recognized as one of the best guide dog schools in the country, and the number of applicants far exceeded their capacity to train and deploy qualified teams of dogs and students.

In August, 1973, the board of directors elected Duke R. Lee, Jr., a Grand Lodge Representative from IAM District 94, to serve a one year term as President.

Lee was fifty-six-years-old, six feet tall and Hollywood flamboyant. He was the son of "Big Duke" Lee, a cowboy who performed with Buffalo Bill Cody's Wild West Show and the Miller Brother's 101 Ranch and Wild West Show before becoming a Hollywood movie actor who appeared in nearly a hundred western films between 1913 and 1946. Duke junior rode in some of the same shows as a boy, and was dubbed "Little Duke."

Little Duke had grown up in Hollywood in its early years and had extensive ties in the community and the entertainment industry. When acting didn't work out for him, he got a job as an inspector at Flying Tigers Freight Service and became active in the IAM. He was also an Exalted Grand Ruler of the Burbank Elks, a member of the Los Angeles Junior Chamber of Commerce, and a Vice President of the Los Angeles County Federation of Labor.

Duke Lee quickly decided that things were too crowded at the Denny Avenue facility and moved the IGE administrative offices to a building on Cahuenga Boulevard, about a half mile away, right across the street from the Los Angeles Acting School.

He used his considerable energies to convince the board that the position of President of IGE should be full-time, and began advocating for a new, larger training facility.

Guiding Eyes
GL⬤BE

Vol. 1, No. 2   Sylmar, California   Spring, 1982

Duke Lee, President Emeritus, with long-time friend "Iron Eyes" Cody
(Story Inside)

The board approved Lee's suggestion to make the presidency a fulltime position, and somewhat reluctantly gave him the go-ahead to begin the search for a bigger campus – if he could raise the money.

What followed was a whirlwind of activity that resulted in a spectacular new home for International Guiding Eyes, but very nearly destroyed the organization in the process.

One of his first schemes was to hold a dog show, a natural for an organization that provided scientifically trained dogs, he figured. The response was overwhelming and chaotic. More than 1,200 dogs and their owners showed up, completely overwhelming the small Denny Avenue facility. After a full afternoon of trying to maintain order and sort things out, Judge Earl Gullikson from the American Kennel Club declared "Puff N Stuff," a Pekingese owned by a local resident the winner. The event, which IGE moved to a city park in subsequent years to avoid the same circus like atmosphere, proved a success financially, raising $4,000 for IGE. [1]

Next, he sent the IGE trainers off-campus to begin teaching basic obedience classes for domestic dogs that would never be guide dogs for the visually impaired. That gambit raised a few dollars for IGE and did nothing to improve Lee's relationship with the professional staff. [2]

IGE was still receiving considerable financial support from the IAM and from organizations such as the Lockheed "Buck of the Month Club," which donated another $11,000 in 1973, but if he wanted his new campus he would have to come up with more money. [3]

Patty Gibbons, an IGE graduate who worked at the school with her guide "Ginger" found out that the aluminum pull tabs from beer and soft drink cans could be redeemed for ten cents a pound as scrap metal and began a collection campaign. It took twenty tons of cans and tabs to raise the $4,000 it cost to train a guide dog, but the notion of helping spread like wildfire and soon small articles appeared in newspapers across the country encouraging people to send their pull tabs to IGE. The result was a mountain of pull tabs arriving at IGE every day by mail and delivery truck.

Jonathan Winters, a movie star and comedian, took a fancy to the notion and posed for publicity shots with a wagon load of cans and pull tabs, a puppy, and an IGE graduate accompanied by her dog. [4]

Winters was so impressed with the work of IGE that he agreed to become an Honorary Chairman. He took an active role in IGE activities and did his best to promote Lee's many fundraising schemes which expanded to include a "Bike-A-Thon," complete with

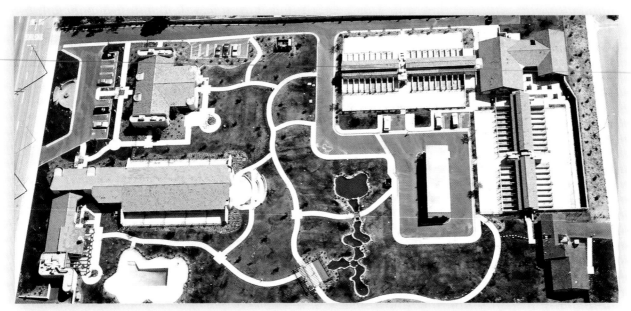

Aerial view of the Guide Dogs of America Sylmar campus.

a guest appearance by "Lassie," celebrity auctions featuring popular entertainers such as television star Tim Conway, a newspaper collection drive by Junior Women's Clubs, and even an Arabian horse show.

The long search for a location that would give IGE adequate space and allow for scores of dogs to live on campus finally paid off in early 1975, when a scenic seven and a half acre site was found in Sylmar, fourteen miles north of the Denny Avenue facility.

A groundbreaking ceremony was held in the spring of 1975, and soon the sound of bulldozers and chain saws echoed through Wilson Canyon as the site began to take shape.

Unfortunately, the economy of the United States was in recession in the mid-1970 with high unemployment, rampant inflation and skyrocketing gasoline prices. Fundraising slowed to a crawl, and the grandiosity of the plan Duke Lee had sold to the IGE Board of Directors became clear. Construction proved to be problematic in Sylmar's rocky terrain. "We had all kinds of problems during construction," recalled M. E. "Bud" Melvin, a board member at the time who would eventually take over as President of IGE. [5]

The biggest problem proved to be financial. About half way through construction, the funds dried up and work ground to a halt. "For months the construction just laid there," Melvin said, "there was no work at all and it was only half completed." [6]

As Joseph Jones had done thirty years before, Duke Lee turned to the IAM for help in the darkest hours of International Guiding Eyes.

His timing was excellent. The IAM had just elected William W. Winpisinger to be its International President, and "Wimpy," as he was affectionately known, was a man of action.

Wimpy and the IAM helped secure the money to get the project back on track, and after a second groundbreaking ceremony attended by Los Angeles Mayor Tom Bradley, the new facility was finally heading toward completion.

International Guiding Eyes honored Winpisinger as their "Humanitarian of the Year" in 1978, at a Washington, D.C. fundraising banquet where race team owner Roger Penske and Eastern Airlines President Frank Borman were also recognized.

Winpisinger accepted the award graciously and thanked IGE, saying: "It is fitting that the IAM, which grew out of men's need for dignity, has helped create and support independence for others through International Guiding Eyes." [7]

Six long years after the initial groundbreaking, IGE's new school opened on Glenoaks Boulevard in Sylmar on July 1, 1981. ●

Duke Lee (kneeling) restored the IGE Presidency to a full time position, but his ambitions and overreaching nearly bankrupted the school.

Chapter 9
Rebound

William W. Winpisinger was a transitional figure who had a profound impact on the IAM and everything they were involved with, including International Guiding Eyes. An automobile mechanic by trade, he was a native of Cleveland who dropped out of high school, fought

Bud Melvin inherited a school that cost seventy thousand dollars a month to operate, but had only seven thousand dollars in the bank. His turnaround of the school was nothing short of remarkable.

He encouraged Melvin, a 52 year old railroad machinist who had worked his way up from the floor of the Santa Fe Railroad roundhouse in Los Angeles to the position of General Chairman of District Lodge 19, to assume the presidency of IGE and asked him to do everything he could to

in World War II aboard a landing ship that was at Normandy Beach on D-Day, and came up through the ranks of one of the largest and fastest growing unions in the country.

Wimpy, as he was known, began his Presidency of the IAM with a midnight staff meeting to announce that a new day was dawning for the union. He wanted to revamp and revitalize every aspect of the sprawling organization, and that included reaffirming the IAM's commitment to IGE.

"Wimpy felt deeply about making sure International Guiding Eyes was a success," recalled George Kourpias, Winpisinger's closest confidant and himself a future president of the IAM. "He had been to California and seen the dogs, the students, and the trainers. He came back and told me that we had to do something to help improve the school." [1]

As he worked his way up through the ranks of the IAM, Winpisinger had accumulated a trusted band of operatives, all self-made men who were loyal to one another, hard charging, and dedicated to the IAM: George Kourpias, Phil Zannella, Frank Souza, and Bud Melvin.

turn International Guiding Eyes around.

Melvin recalled his sometimes unorthodox communication with Wimpy: "He'd get into his office in Washington at seven thirty or eight in the morning and give me a call. Well, that's four thirty or five o'clock West Coast time. I'd be lying in bed, and he'd bellow: 'Are you up yet?' and I'd reply: 'Does laying in bed *at attention* count?" [2]

Melvin was already serving as one of the members of the board of directors of IGE, and at Winpisinger's urging agreed to go to work at the school and be ready to take over when Duke Lee retired. Like many of his fellow board members, Melvin was concerned that Duke Lee had overextended the organization by pushing for the new facility and letting fundraising take a back seat. Several of Lee's latest fundraising schemes, including a dinner in Hawaii that didn't even raise enough money to offset costs, had fallen flat and it was becoming more and more obvious that a significant change was needed.

Duke Lee was still President, but was spending less and less time at the office as he neared retirement. Melvin was shunted off to a small office at the rear of the new headquarters but from where he sat he got a complete view of the shape of the organization, and he didn't like what he saw. IGE was under the strain of an enormous mortgage on the new Sylmar property. Fundraising was lagging, and staff morale was at an all time low. As he bided his time until Lee's eventual retirement, Melvin began to formulate a plan of action.

When he was finally elected President in 1982, Melvin inherited an organization that cost seventy thousand dollars a month to operate, but had only seven thousand dollars in the bank. He was forced to take drastic measures to meet the payroll and keep the lenders at bay, including sending staff members from store to store to collect the spare change in the Heidi banks.

One of the problems was that the property on Denny Avenue in North Hollywood that had served as IGE headquarters before completion of the Sylmar campus was still on the market. Melvin approached Winpisinger and asked for a loan for operating capital, offering the North Hollywood property as collateral. Winpisinger agreed, and the IAM Executive Council voted to lend IGE two hundred thousand dollars to keep it afloat.

Given some breathing room, Melvin began to implement his turnaround plan. He found a new agent to market the North Hollywood property, and within a few months it was sold and the IAM was repaid. He ramped up fundraising and worked hard to improve the morale of the staff.

Melvin recalled the uncertainty he faced in those early days: "I'd wake up at two or three o'clock in the morning, make myself a cup of coffee and sit at my dining room table just thinking things through. It got so bad at one point I actually considered bankruptcy, but thankfully it never came to that." [3]

Melvin consulted with professional fundraisers who suggested hosting a big dinner honoring someone as a means of getting people involved and attracting sponsors. He called Winpisinger and asked if he would be willing to be the guest of honor on his birth-

day. Wimpy agreed, and Melvin was off and running.

He scheduled the dinner at Caesar's Palace in Las Vegas, and allotted each of the top IAM leaders a block of tickets to sell, pitting them against one another to see who could be the best salesman. This also gave him the chance to ask IGE's corporate donors to participate and he made sure that the people from Boeing knew just how much the people from Lockheed were contributing so that they would both get equal recognition in the program book. He immersed himself in the workings of the dinner, selecting the food, finding the entertainment, arranging the speaking program and developing the seating chart. No detail was too small for his attention. Then he did something unheard of – he encouraged people *not* to come to the dinner. Each dinner guest rightfully expected to be fed, and all those meals cost money. The folks who bought a ticket but stayed home represented pure profit.

When the dinner was held there were two hundred people in the room, but IGE had sold more than five hundred tickets. International Guiding Eyes raised more than a hundred thousand dollars at a cost of less than ten thousand dollars, a return any professional fundraiser would view with envy. A new day had dawned for IGE fundraising.

Winpisinger did his part to help revitalize fundraising. In addition to attaching his name to the dinner, Wimpy instructed his communications staff to go all-out to stimulate IAM support. Soon, an article appeared in *The Machinist* announcing: "Guiding Eyes' Dog Crusade Opens." The article, which featured pictures of the new Sylmar facility, dogs, students, and a clip-out coupon titled "I'll Help Others See," concluded with the pitch: "To help IGE carry out its humanitarian efforts, the IAM is calling on all members, locals, districts and business leaders across the USA and Canada to contribute to this worthwhile project. Numerous fund-raising programs are being planned." [4]

Melvin worked hard to cultivate the donor base and began putting the organization's financial

balance sheets in their annual report, something the previous leadership had been loath to do. He joined every social club and service organization in the Greater Los Angeles area, and asked to be put on their speaking program. Soon, donations and fundraising ideas were flowing in from the Elks, Eagles, Moose and Chamber of Commerce.

He arranged to have Cliff Robertson, a popular movie star, appear in and narrate a short video about International Guiding Eyes, called "*Partners.*" In the piece, students and their guide dogs are shown riding a city bus, checking in at the airport, and going through a normal day at the office. The new Sylmar campus is shown off to great advantage, and the migration from German Shepherds to Labrador Retrievers and Golden Retrievers as the dogs of choice to be trained as guides is explained. The video was made available to the many service organizations Melvin belonged to and was offered to IAM lodges across the US and Canada. It proved to be a great fundraising tool.

The biggest hurdle IGE faced was still the monthly carrying cost for the mortgage on their new school. Winpisinger and the IAM agreed to assume the mortgage and let Guiding Eyes pay back the cost without interest. Wimpy secured the necessary funds from a Texas based insurance company run by a friend of his and with the lower carrying cost and better fundraising, International Guiding Eyes began to turn the corner.

Bud Melvin's wife, Virginia, recalled one of those early morning calls from Winpisinger. "Wimpy called first thing in the morning," Virginia Melvin said, "and I told him Bud was so worried about IGE that he wasn't sleeping. He said to me, 'That's funny, since Bud's been running the place, *I've* been sleeping like a baby.'" [5]

Melvin had been on the job two years by the time he was asked to address the IAM's Grand Lodge Convention in September of 1984, and he had a considerable amount of good news to report to the delegates.

"Since the beginning in 1948, when they trained one dog at a time, we have placed one thousand five hundred dogs with the blind from all over the world. We furnish them regardless of race, color, creed, sex, age, national origin or religious belief." [6]

He then related the story of four Israeli soldiers who had been blinded in the 1982 war in Lebanon, during a mission known as "Operation Peace for Galilee." The soldiers were flown to Sylmar where one of the assistant trainers was an Israeli who was learning to teach dogs to guide so that he could open a guide dog school in Israel. With that trainer's help in their native language, and dogs bought with IAM donations, the soldiers from one of America's staunchest allies were able to return home and lead better lives.

The delegates cheered news of progress at IGE, and then the IAM's General Secretary Treasurer, Tom Ducy, informed Melvin that the members of Local Lodge 1916 in Milwaukee, where General Electric Corporation manufactured X-Ray machines, had convinced the company to allow them to refurbish a machine on their own time and donate it to IGE for use in their veterinary clinic, a donation that was worth more than sixty thousand dollars.

The IAM continued to do all they could to help raise funds for the school. The union offered a calendar for sale each year, an item that was very popular with its members. Wimpy directed that seventy-five cents of the cover price of each two dollar calendar – essentially their entire profit margin – be donated to IGE. With a yearly volume of nearly 100,000 calendars, that brought in close to $75,000 for IGE.

Melvin then managed to get the US Government to recognize IGE as an official charity eligible for donations from the Combined Federal Campaign, a government-wide program where employees were able to choose among charities to receive voluntary contributions deducted from their paychecks each month. Winpisinger immediately fired off a letter to each IAM local at government facilities strongly encouraging them to designate IGE as their charity of choice.

An unexpected windfall helped stabilize the financial situation when Margaret Pallack, an 87 year-old heiress to an iron and steel industry fortune, bequeathed $525,000 to IGE in her will. That represented the largest individual contribution to date to IGE, and Miss Pallack's generosity was marked with a special bronze plaque in the Guiding Eyes Court of Honor near its main entrance.

Melvin continued the IGE tradition of involving the Hollywood community in support of the school, and over the course of a few years, actors David Hasselhoff and Heather Thomas posed with IGE puppies; Elizabeth Montgomery filmed a television movie called "*Second Sight, A Love Story*" – about a blind woman who finds a new lease on life due to her guide dog "Emma;" Betty White hosted a celebrity chili cook-off; and actress Cheryl McMannis, herself an IGE graduate, took a very active role in promoting the school.

The donations of Hollywood stars, corporations, service clubs and individuals who gave everything from their spare change in a Heidi Bank to a half million dollar bequeath in their will were lifting IGE financially, but the support of the IAM was still critically important to the organization. By the time Melvin addressed the IAM's centennial Grand Lodge Convention in Atlanta in May, 1988, he was able to report remarkable results from the renewed partnership between IGE and the IAM.

"In 1984, I told you that we brought in about $800,000," Melvin said to the assembled delegates. "I'm happy to tell you that this fiscal year we brought in a million, four hundred thousand. In 1982, we graduated a total of nine students. This year we will graduate sixty-four, and we have seventy-two scheduled to graduate next year." [7]

Throughout his term as IGE President, Melvin continued to find bigger and better ways to raise funds and promote the school. His friend Frank Souza started a golf tournament in Oakland, California, that became an annual event. Motorcycle enthusiasts

Actress Betty White has supported IGE and Guide Dogs of America for more than three decades.

began an annual ride they dubbed "Hawgs for Dawgs" in 1990, and before long the event was contributing a considerable amount to IGE each year.

Each year, the proceeds from the calendar sales, golf tournaments, motorcycle rides and other fundraising activities grew and grew, and by 1990, the annual Winpisinger Dinner was bringing in close to $300,000.

Lockheed's "Buck of the Month Club," the Combined Federal Campaign and regular donations from a broad range of service organizations rounded out what had become a very successful fundraising operation.

As proud as he was of the financial rebound, Melvin was even more proud of another statistic: International Guiding Eyes was now graduating sixty teams of guide dogs and students each year. The school that had slowed to a crawl in the early 1980's had come roaring back and was poised for a bright future. ●

IGE and Guide Dogs of America has had a display at every large function sponsored by the IAM for many years, and has always enjoyed the support of its members.

IGE President Bud Melvin (left) gets a laugh at close friend Phil Zannella (center) who shows he's given every cent in his pocket to IGE.

Executives from General Dynamics present IGE President Bud Melvin (left) with surgical equipment for the IGE veterinary lab in 1985.

Melvin and IAM President William W. Winpisinger talk with an IGE staff member at the Sylmar campus.

Melvin, IAM General Secretary Treasurer Gene Glover, and William "Wimpy" Winpisinger, the IAM International President.

Chapter 10
Guide Dogs of America

Bud Melvin had one more major contribution to make to International Guiding Eyes before he retired, and it would have a profound impact on the entire organization. Melvin was troubled by the fact that the name "International Guiding Eyes," seemed to be inhibiting fundraising. He described the situation in a speech to the 1992 Grand Lodge Convention of the IAM.

"In the federal sector, they have a program called the CFC," Melvin told the delegates meeting in Montreal, Canada. "That's Combined Federal Campaigns, and that's the United Way for all federal bases, army bases, the Bureau of Printing and Engraving in Washington, DC, and all your federal buildings throughout the nation. They all give to CFC. It is a mandatory designation and you're allowed to designate to your charity if the charity is listed.

So, we asked the federal employees to give to CFC. We had a little program here and we started about four years ago, and we got forty thousand dollars from the CFC campaign. And one of our sister guide dog

schools, there's ten in the nation, the one from Long Island called the Guide Dog Foundation, they were about ten thousand ahead of us. And the next year, we brought in seventy thousand and thought we were doing good, and they were further ahead of us.

And then I went out with John Meese, and we visited all the bases. We went everywhere, the shipyards, and the military bases, and we ran campaigns and we gave out posters and we did all kinds of things, and we're up to a hundred and fifty thousand, and that guy sitting at his desk on Long Island is up to seven hundred and fifty thousand!

So we ran a survey to find out what the hell's going on here. We're working the field and the money's going to somebody else. Well, number one, they're listed just four numbers ahead of us, which can be part of it. But the people running the analysis for us out of Washington, DC, took people and said 'What do you think the name International Guiding Eyes means?'

Well, the most popular answer was something

to do with eye surgery or transplants in Third World countries. It's a volunteer thing. Guide dog work ended up fourth or fifth on their choices. So the board of directors voted last month to start another name, and we will be doing business as Guide Dogs of America." [1]

Melvin also reported to the delegates on the continuing progress and prosperity of what would henceforth be Guide Dogs of America, including a new and exciting relationship with Texas Agriculture and Mining University for a genetic testing program for the dogs.

"We have records of dogs for forty years," Melvin said, "from the time they were born until the time they pass away, and all their illnesses and their problems in the interim. Texas A&M is doing a genetic study. They are marking DNA markers, genomes, they're called, and if they find the marker in the DNA that says this dog is carrying or has hip dysplasia or whatever, they can take a blood test of the dog and if they have any of the undesirable traits, then you don't breed the dog, and your success rate is going to jump by thirty percent." [2]

Melvin then announced that through the IAM he had found a donor willing to underwrite the quarter million dollars the study would cost. He introduced Houston attorney Weldon Granger, a generous man who had supported the IAM and IGE for years, to the roaring approval of the delegates.

Granger made brief remarks and was afforded a standing ovation.

Showing the pluck that had allowed him to take an organization that was millions of dollars in debt and on the verge of extinction and breathe new life into so that it was again a going concern with millions of dollars of assets, Melvin turned to Granger as he began to take his seat.

"Weldon," Melvin said, "I'll get you another standing ovation for another quarter of a million. What do you say?" [3]

Granger politely demurred, but over the course of the coming decades he and his family would indeed donate many times that amount to the organization that now proudly called itself Guide Dogs of America. ●

Chapter 11
A Modern Guide Dog School

The Winpisinger Dinner in Las Vegas has become a mainstay of Guide Dogs of America fundraising efforts.

John Petttitt became President of Guide Dogs of America when Bud Melvin retired in 1992. He had been a staff member of the IAM for nearly three decades, and his charge was to maintain and grow what was now a mature organization, with a modern training facility, an experienced professional staff, and a steady stream of income.

He continued the tradition of involving Hollywood personalities in Guide Dogs of America, and convinced British actor Dudley Moore, star of the hit film *"Arthur,"* to do a promotional video. The fifteen minute film was called *"Partners,"* and stressed the special relationship between students at GDA and their canine guides.

During Pettitt's administration Guide Dogs of America added an in-home training program for students who were getting replacement guides, and completed work on a new puppy nursery that allowed GDA to insulate their puppies from germs and other risks that were associated with housing them with the mature dogs.

The highlight of Pettitt's presidency was making the final payment on the mortgage for the Sylmar campus. The IAM had rescued Guide Dogs of America in 1982, by issuing an interest-free loan in the amount of $2.5 million, saving the organization a total of $1.3 million in interest payments over the term of the loan. With a final payment of $98,701.62, in September, 1996, the debt was paid in full, and Guide Dogs of America was able to hold a ceremony to burn the mortgage documents.

Guide Dogs of America marked its fiftieth anniversary in 1998, with the usual cake, balloons and fanfare. The program that started when a blind machinist from Mississippi was denied a guide dog because he was "too old" at age fifty-seven, had blossomed into an institution that had given the gift of sight through scientifically trained guide dogs to more than a thousand people of all ages, races, and walks of life free of charge, and had done so without ever taking money from the government.

As Pettitt neared retirement the board of directors began to search for a suitable person to take the helm. They found him in Jay Bormann, a fifty-one year old Grand Lodge Field Auditor for the IAM. Bormann was born in Oregon and early in his career worked at Portland Iron Works, Reynolds Aluminum and Boeing. He rose through the ranks of his IAM local to become President of District 24, and was appointed to the staff of the international where he developed a specialty of closing out units that were economically distressed or no longer necessary because of mergers. When Tom Buffenbarger, the International President of the IAM and a key board member of GDA, called Bormann about taking the position there was a bit of initial confusion.

"I thought maybe I was being sent out there to close things up and liquidate it," Bormann said later. "I kind of got it in my mind that what he wanted was for me to go in and do a closure. It couldn't have been further from the truth. When I said that to Tom Buffenbarger he just laughed at me and said he wanted just the opposite, he wanted me to *grow* the organization." [1]

With that mandate Bormann set off on what he described as a tremendous learning curve.

"The business aspect of it was easy," Bormann said, "it was the rule of the prudent man: would you do this with your own money? And that's how I operated, if I wouldn't spend my own money on it, I wasn't going to spend someone else's. But the dog aspect and the people aspect were much more difficult. Even though I had some experience with people who were visually impaired and had been in a blindfold when I was in high school, nothing can prepare a sighted person for what's in store for them when they start working in that venue. It's really quite startling. If you're sighted, you really have no idea how fortunate you are until you're not sighted." [2]

Naturally, being the President of a guide dog school meant spending a lot of time around dogs, and Bormann, who admitted an affinity for cats, was happy to delegate that aspect to the professionals. "I stayed away from the dogs," Bormann said. I had people who knew everything there was to know about dogs, and they didn't need me for anything." [3]

Instead he used his time to improve living conditions at the school, build community support,

IAM President George Kourpias continued the tradition of supporting IGE.

strengthen the ties of the school with the various elements of the guide dog community, and raise more money to keep GDA afloat.

Under Bormann, Guide Dogs of America stepped up its relationship with police departments, fire departments and other service groups by giving them highly trained dogs that could not make the cut to be a guide dog. Those animals were re-tasked for roles such as cadaver dogs, bomb sniffing dogs, drug sniffing dogs, and therapy dogs.

Bormann also used his administrative skills to usher Guide Dogs of America into the digital age, installing the first computer system and developing the first web page.

Reflecting on his tenure as GDA president, Bormann was most proud of the people who comprised the guide dog community. He expressed special gratitude to the volunteer puppy raisers: "No guide dog school could stay in business without them" Bormann said. "I realized very quickly that with two hundred and fifty puppies a year being raised that that's a lot of socks, shoes and bones being chewed on and a lot of miscues on the floor to clean up. And some of those people have raised fifteen or twenty puppies for us. We couldn't do it without them." [4]

Bormann had tremendous success doing what Tom Buffenbarger asked of him, growing the organization. By the time he reached retirement age, he had

IAM President Tom Buffenbarger listens as Guide Dogs of America President Jay Bormann speaks at the 2005 Winpisinger Dinner.

substantially increased the school's endowment, had a top flight professional staff, and was turning out a steady stream of highly trained guide dogs.

He refused to accept all the credit himself, and instead insisted that the reason Guide Dogs of America had become so successful was because of the donors and volunteers who made it all possible.

"Those people are phenomenal," Bormann said. "They understand the program, they give until it hurts, and they work incredibly hard, just because it's the right thing to do." [5]

When Bormann retired in 2009, the Guide Dogs of America Board of Directors selected Dale E. Hartford, a fifty-three-year-old staff member of the IAM to lead the organization. Hartford grew up in Maine, where he studied to become a marine engineer. He practiced his trade as a millwright-welder at the S.D. Warren Paper Company, in Skowhegan, Maine, where he joined the union. He served as the Directing Business Representative of IAM District 99, and was appointed to the international staff of

the union in 1986, where he rose to the position of Administrative Assistant to the General Vice President of the Eastern Territory.

At Guide Dogs of America, Hartford continued in the tradition of Jay Bormann, strengthening ties with volunteers, staff, puppy raisers and donors, and set in motion an ambitious program to improve the facilities at Sylmar.

He also constructed a new area for the school's graduations and installed a "puppy cam" to allow donors and others to view the cuddly little future guide dogs in the school's puppy nursery.

Commenting on the selection of Hartford, IAM International President Tom Buffenbarger said: "The Board of Guide Dogs of America wanted someone who could lead and grow what is now a very successful program. I believe we found just the right person in Dale Hartford. His drive and determination set the pace for meeting our mission of serving the visually impaired by giving them the gift of sight." [6]

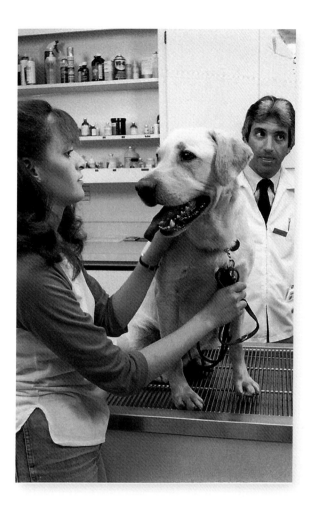

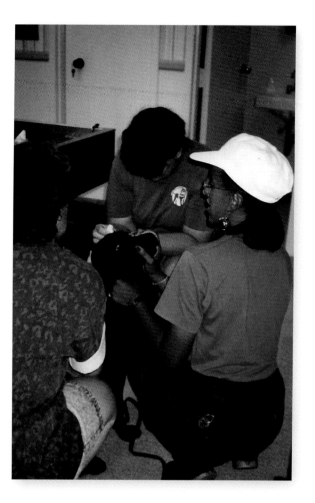

John Pettitt (second from left) became President of GDA when Bud Melvin retired. He is shown here with AFL-CIO Secretary Treasurer Richard Trumka (left) and AFL-CIO President John Sweeney (second from right).

Why These Breeds?

The first guide dogs were exclusively German Shepherds, and in the case of International Guiding Eyes, exclusively female German Shepherds. Today several breeds of dog of both genders are used, with the Labrador Retriever, Golden Retriever, and German Shepherd being the most common, in that order.

Chuck Jordan, Director of Programs for Guide Dogs of America, who has been training dogs and guide dogs for more than forty years, explains the evolution:

"There have been many breeds of dogs that have been trained to do guide work, but can you get a group ready for a group of people? You have to stick with breeds that will give you the flexibility – size wise, temperament wise, and strength wise – and will be able to adapt to climates from Southern California to Maine, from Texas to Washington state.

Training dogs to lead blind people developed in Germany at the end of World War I, so the German Shepherd was a natural choice. When it evolved in this country in the late 1920's with The Seeing Eye, it was with 'Buddy,' one of Dorothy Eustace's shepherds.

Shepherds were used almost exclusively, and female shepherds at this school, and they were very good.

But if you stop and look, not at the dogs, but at the people, and blindness as a disability, from the 1920's on up through the mid 1950's, not much was available. Kids were put in schools for the blind, and adults who didn't have families to care for them were put in 'Light Houses for the Blind.' They were custodial care institutions.

At the end of World War II, in 1948, Dr. Hines, a Navy Lieutenant Junior Grade, was put in charge of a wing of 300 blinded veterans with the goal of getting them off their duff and out of the hospital. He developed a means of teaching people to use long white canes as an independent way of traveling. From 1948 through the 1950's, this became known as 'Orientation Mobility,' and was being taught as a science.

The first graduating class of qualified Mobility Specialists graduated in 1960. So then you had agencies becoming truly rehabilitative instead of being focused on custodial care. They were teaching people how to get out and travel and find jobs other than door to door sales. And that's where the shepherds fit in. Prior to this time, most of the people who got guide dogs were self taught, self motivated, and usually self employed doing some form of door to door sales, Fuller Brushes, magazine subscriptions, or what have you. Most of them were men, between the ages of twenty and forty-five.

In that period shepherds worked well. In 1960, with the development of Orientation Mobility, and instructors being sent out we started getting, throughout the industry, applications from other types of people. No longer were they just the 'John Wayne's' of blindom, they were normal people, they were housewives with three kids, they were older folks, a whole range of people with differing needs.

In 1957, diabetes became the leading cause of blindness. Up until then it had been glaucoma. And with the diabetes came a very serious, physically limiting disease, particularly back when they didn't have the medications to control it.

So they needed some gentler dogs. The younger blind people were being mainstreamed, put into regular schools and being encouraged to go to college. So they had hours and hours of sitting in classrooms. Well, the shepherd is a strong, hard charging six to seven miles a day type worker. When you lay them down and they don't get a chance to burn that energy, it can manifest itself in a hyperkinetic misbehavior.

So, they looked at the Golden Retriever. The Golden Retriever, as a breed of dog, is the *oppo-*

Chuck Jordan, Director of Programs for Guide Dogs of America.

site of the German Shepherd. They're very loving and very sweet. They can be silly and goofy and playful, but they're very kind dogs. They don't require a lot of physical management. They're ready to go for a walk if you want to walk, but if you don't want to leave your house for a week, they're okay with that too.

The Labrador Retriever was kind of between the two. Not as active and demanding as the shepherd, but not as laid back and easygoing as the golden retriever. So they gave us a variety of traits to match with people's lifestyles.

As the years progressed and more and more people were rehabilitated, we started seeing less and less of the 'John Wayne' types and more and more normal people with normal needs.

All three breeds have a real serious willingness and desire to please. So many breeds are smart, but they see no benefit in pleasing you. These three breeds were selected because their I.Q.'s are about the same, meaning they learn at about the same rate of speed and they retain it.

The Labrador Retrievers started taking over because as a breed of dog they're a little bit more versatile in terms of what they can do. Their coat is easier to maintain, because it's a short flat coat, but a double coat that protects them in the summer heat or the cold of winter. So over the last thirty years, in every country, labs have become the breed that's used most today."

PART II

The Guide Dog Process

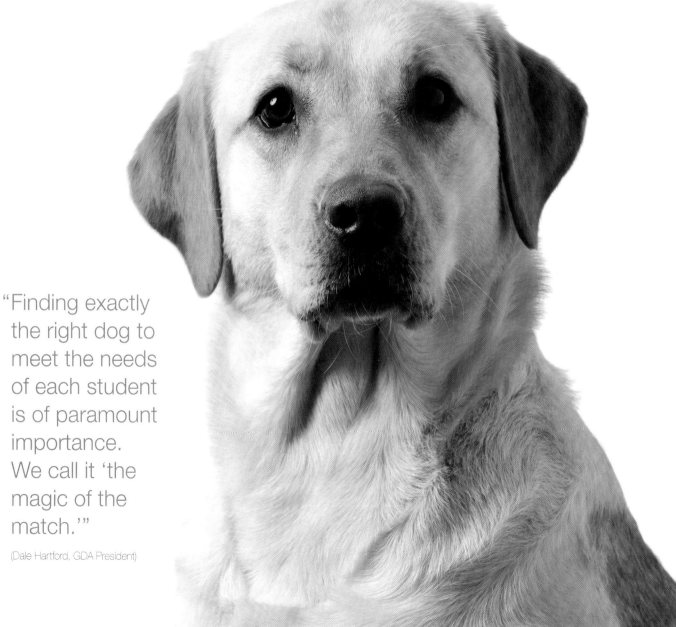

"Finding exactly the right dog to meet the needs of each student is of paramount importance. We call it 'the magic of the match.'"

(Dale Hartford, GDA President)

Chapter 12
Breeding

For many years International Guiding Eyes trained only female German Shepherds to be guide dogs. They did not have their own breeding program, and depended upon people to donate dogs to be trained as guides. This saved the school the cost of raising puppies, but it took a great deal of effort to find a sufficient number of dogs to meet the needs of their students, and the success rate of finding dogs that had the necessary intelligence and were physically and temperamentally suitable ran

Actress Amanda Righetti, GDA celebrity spokesperson.

well below fifty percent. That meant a lot of time was wasted testing dogs who were not ever going to be matched with a human partner.

In 1981, the school decided to begin its own breeding program to develop a more reliable stock of puppies.

Today, Guide Dogs of America has a very successful breeding program that produces approximately 200 puppies each year. The policy of training just female German Shepherds has given way to a program that accepts dogs of both genders from a stock of Labrador Re-

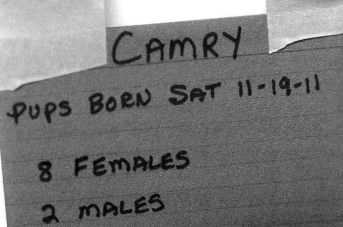

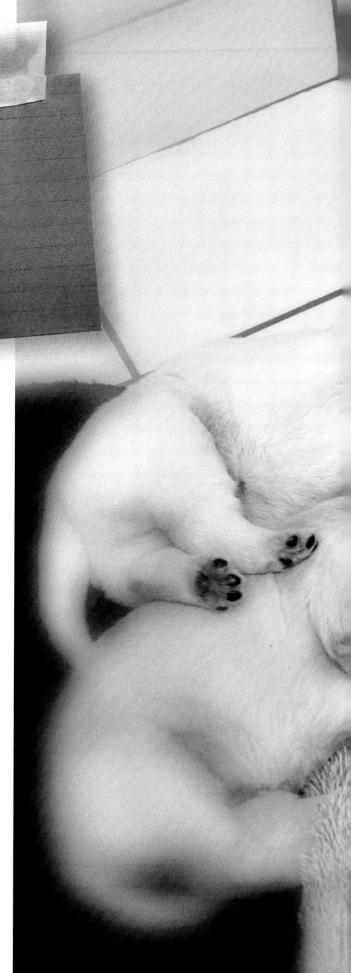

trievers, Golden Retrievers and German Shepherds.

For the most part the breeder dogs come from the school's own line, but occasionally they will accept dogs donated from the lines of other guide dog schools or from reputable breeders to lower the prospect of inbreeding. In those cases, careful attention is paid to pedigree, temperament, and joint and eye health.

Female dogs are bred once each year, and male breed dogs usually are bred four times a year.

This program allows Guide Dogs of America to plan ahead in two year cycles to assure that they have a sufficient stock of dogs to meet the needs of incoming students and to replace older guide dogs that have reached the end of their productive years as guides.

The school's breeding department is kept separate from the main kennel and puppies are maintained in a sterile environment to prevent the introduction of any germs or viruses while they are being weaned.

The majority of births are through the natural process, and a veterinarian technician is on twenty-four hour a day call to provide immediate assistance in case there are any complications during pregnancy or delivery. ●

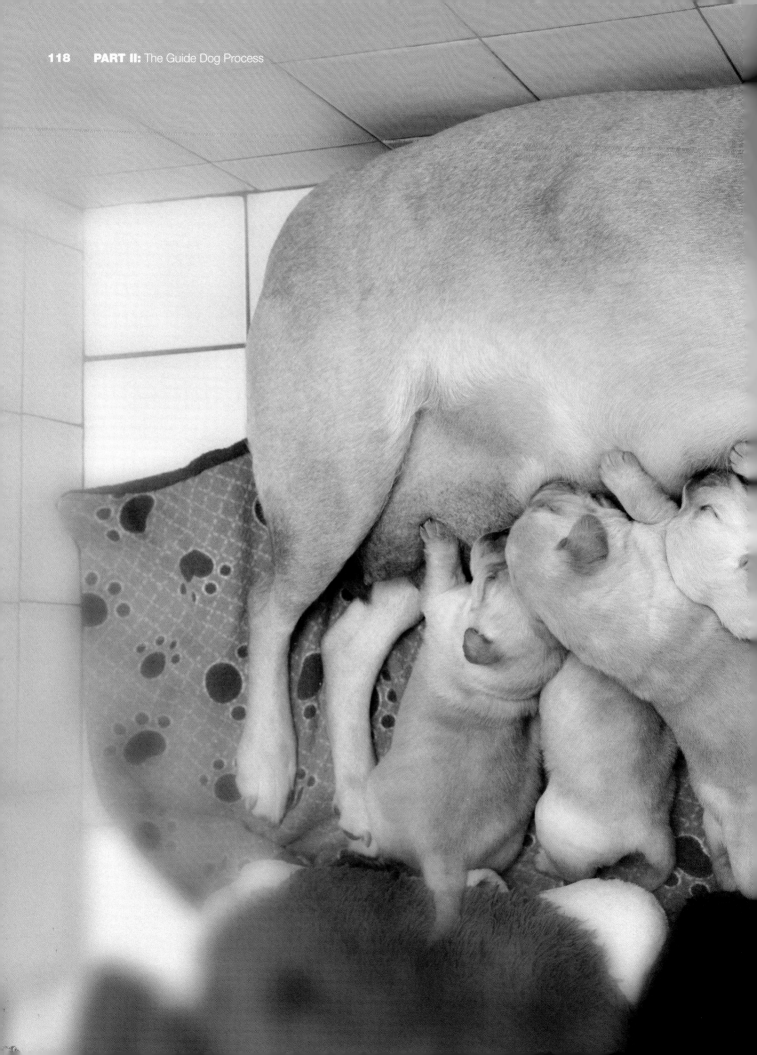

Meri Forman, GDA Puppy Nursery.

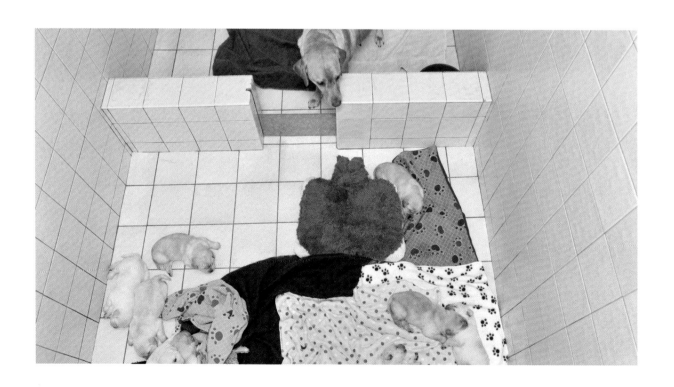

Chapter 13
Puppy Department

Louise Henderson, GDA Puppy Department.

Once the puppies are weaned and ready to leave the nursery, the Puppy Department springs into action.

Staff of the Puppy Department arrange for the dogs to be placed with volunteers who will raise the puppy for the next twelve to fourteen months. The process begins with GDA staff interviewing prospective puppy raisers, and if the interview goes well, a home inspection. The staff plays careful attention to the environment where the puppy will be raised, checking for safety, making sure the volunteer can devote sufficient time to the puppy, and determining the household situation. They prefer an active environment with children and other pets, including cats, to help acclimate the puppy to the many distractions they will face if they make the successful transition to becoming a guide dog.

Guide Dogs of America usually has three hundred puppies out with volunteer puppy rais-

ers at any given time. They group them into nine geographic areas, with clusters in California from San Louis Obispo to San Diego, and individual groups in Washington State and Montana.

At the outset of the program, puppies were tracked by slips of paper with the volunteer's name and telephone number and not much more information. The slips of paper were tacked to a bulletin board, and when the allotted time had gone by someone would call the volunteer and ask them to bring the dog in for training.

Today, each puppy has a microchip implanted in their ear before they leave the GDA campus. A sophisticated computer tracking program is used to monitor the progress of all puppies, and with the click of a mouse the staff of the Puppy Department can call up each dog's medical records, vital signs, weight, medications, test results, and family history.

The Puppy Department holds puppy raiser classes to train people new to the program, and each puppy is evaluated at least twice while they are in the volunteer's home. Any problems with the puppy's training are identified at that point, and suggestions for corrective action are offered by GDA staff.

Each puppy comes with a vaccination schedule, and the puppy raiser is responsible for making sure the vaccinations are administered either at Guide Dogs of America or by a qualified veterinarian.

New volunteers to be puppy raisers are always welcome, and the staff of the Puppy Department visit meetings and conventions to explain the program and seek new "parents" to help raise the next generation of guide dogs. ●

Chapter 14
Puppy Raising

Judy Reilly, volunteer puppy raiser with "Milo," her ninth puppy for GDA.

Raising the puppies that will eventually become guide dogs is one of the most critical steps in the process. When puppies are weaned, usually seven or eight weeks after they are born, they're placed with specially selected, pre-screened volunteer foster families known as "puppy raisers," who will care for them for the next eighteen to twenty months. Puppy raisers provide their young charges with basic obedience skills, socialization, and a loving environment.

Judy Reilly, a Los Angeles area resident who has raised ten puppies for Guide Dogs of America, explained how she got involved with this worthwhile program.

"I had been volunteering for various organizations," Reilly said, "and I saw an article in the newspaper about how Guide Dogs of America was looking for puppy raisers. I thought to myself: 'this is the best of all possible worlds, I get to do some good and I get to hang out with a *dog* twenty-four, seven!'. My husband

asked if we could take the dog everywhere, and when I told him we could, he said: 'we're in!'" [1]

"Our job as puppy raisers," Reilly continued, "is to do two things. First, we teach the dog basic obedience: sit, stay, come, down…really the basic stuff. More importantly, we socialize them in all types of situations. I don't know who the puppy will be matched with, it could be a farmer in Des Moines or a businessman in Los Angeles, so we have to expose the puppy to as many scenarios as possible. For instance, I don't usually take public transportation, but on occasion I will take the bus just so that the puppy is exposed to that environment, because it's quite possible whoever gets him may have to rely on public transportation." [2]

Guide Dogs of America prefers that puppies be raised in active environments and welcomes volunteers who have children and other pets, including cats.

Many employers will allow puppies in training to accompany their masters to work, but in cases

where that is not allowed and the volunteer works a full schedule, GDA encourages them to consider other volunteer opportunities with the organization. Many future guide dogs are raised in office environments and schools, and people who work from home are always welcome to volunteer.

Although it is somewhat easier for homeowners with backyard space to raise a puppy, Guide Dogs of America also welcomes apartment dwellers to participate, since some of the students who will receive the dogs live in multiunit housing so it's helpful for the puppy to have experienced that.

Each puppy comes with a vaccination schedule of what shots are to be given the dog, and when they are due. If the puppy raiser lives within easy commute of the Sylmar campus they can schedule the vaccinations at the Guide Dogs of America veterinary clinic. If not, they are reimbursed for vaccinations and all other authorized veterinary services the dog receives.

Guide Dogs of America provides puppy raisers with a basic kit when they pick up their young charges, including a leash, collar, identification tag, bowl and a distinctive yellow "Puppy In Training" bib the dog will wear to alert people that this is a special animal.

Judy Reilly recalled her experiences brining Guide Dogs of America puppies in training into locations where dogs are not usually allowed.

"I have an ID," Reilly explained, "and the dog has an ID, and of course he has his bib when he's little and his vest when he's bigger. Generally if you explain to people what you're doing and why the dog is with you, there's rarely a problem. One thing I learned though is that there is no such thing as a quick trip to the grocery store. Everybody wants to talk to you, tell you about their own pets, ask questions about guide dogs, and pet the puppy. It's very good training for the dog, because he has to sit or lie down and behave while all this is going on, but I learned that if I'm in a hurry, its best to leave the dog at home." [3]

The Puppy Department of Guide Dogs of America works closely with the volunteer puppy rais-

"Generally, if you explain what you're doing, there's rarely a problem bringing the puppy into places other dogs aren't allowed," Reilly said.

ers to see that everything goes smoothly. Volunteers are invited to classes at Guide Dogs of America, and each puppy is usually evaluated twice while it's in the puppy raiser's home. Puppy Department staff will advise the puppy raiser of any problems they observe and provide suggestions on how to work through the problem.

About a year and a half after the puppy has gone home with its adoptive family, the puppy raiser receives an invitation to a luncheon at Guide Dogs of America. It's time to bring the young dog in for training.

"We get a letter saying, please come for lunch," Reilly explained. "And they give us a lovely luncheon. There are boxes of Kleenex everywhere, and believe me, they get used. I try to imagine it like the dog's going away to college. You get a little tearful. You spend so much time with them, and you want so badly for them to make it as a guide dog." [4]

The now grown dog is about to undergo a rigorous program of training and testing. If they make it

through, they will be matched with visually impaired partners and will bring joy and mobility to that person. If they do not, they will be offered back to the puppy raiser for full adoption, or they will be refocused to become service dogs of another sort.

If the dog makes it through training and is matched with a visually impaired partner, the volunteer puppy raiser is invited to attend the graduation ceremony. It can be a very emotional experience.

"It's so rewarding," Reilly explained "and thrilling to see your dog again. Once you turn them in for training, you don't see them again for six months. So, you're a little nervous: 'is the dog going to recognize me?' And of course the dog recognizes you, they're all over you, and it's thrilling and exciting to meet their new partner. You meet these people and you immediately see that this dog means so much to them, and that they are clearly in love with that puppy. It's just wonderful to see." [5]

Chapter 15
In For Training

When the luncheon for puppy raisers and their young charges is done, and the emotional good-byes with wagging tails and tearful eyes have been said, the dog is in for training. The hard work that will either make them a guide dog or send them off in another direction as a "career change dog" begins.

First, the dog is given an extensive physical examination by the Guide Dogs of America Veterinarian Department. They are checked for overall health, strength, joint condition and allergies. An ophthalmologist provides a thorough eye examination. Then they are put through another series of evaluations that include a stress test and evaluation of their ability to concentrate and resist distractions.

Some of the factors that could disqualify a dog from guide work include a low willingness to work, nervousness, a high degree of distraction by other animals such as squirrels, cats or other dogs, or fear of traffic.

If the dog passes all of those requirements it is admitted to the training program it will spend the next four to six months working with Guide Dogs of America's professional trainers. Each trainer has completed a three year apprenticeship and has taken a written, oral and practical examination to receive their license from the State of California.

The trainers will work with the dog to instill initiative, hone decision making skills, and teach what is known as "intelligent disobedience," the very specific skill of a guide dog to know that it should disregard a master's command if obeying it would place them in danger – such as a command to proceed off a curb into oncoming traffic that the dog can see, but the master did not hear.

Trainers will use consistency, repetition, and praise as their main tools in shaping the future guide dogs.

The basic requirements of a guide dog's work are the straight line concept, obstacle avoidance, "intelligent disobedience," traffic appreciation, initiative and obedience, and social behavior.

The straight line concept involves training the dog to keep moving in any given direction until they are told to do otherwise by their handler or until it is unable to do so.

Obstacle avoidance teaches the dog to make sure the handler does not come into contact with any object as they move along their path.

Initiative and obedience involves teaching the dog to think and anticipate the handler's actions, while remaining obedient to any actual command. Social behavior skills require the dog to be well behaved and mannerly in any environment or situation.

When the harness is on, guide dogs are all business, but when they're "off duty," they have just as much fun as other dogs.

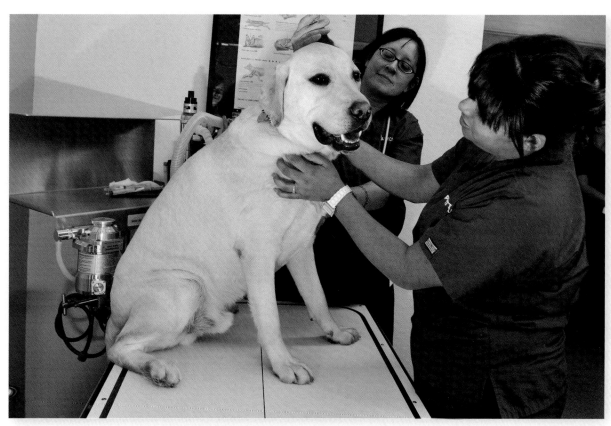

Each guide dog has to meet strict physical requirements to be paired with a human partner.

Puppies have to learn to avoid distractions.

Dogs are put through various scenarios such as indentifying curbs and steps, avoiding traffic, and leading their partners through open spaces or in the midst of crowded sidewalks. Each successful task is rewarded with copious praise, and each "error," or failure to perform exactly as trained, will result in the instructor and dog reworking the scenario over and over until they get it right.

One of the most difficult aspects of guide dog training is teaching the dog to avoid overhangs. Dogs don't naturally look up, and a passage that may be perfectly suitable for them, such as under a scaffold or a low hanging branch, could be disastrous for their taller partner.

Ideally, the dog should guide his partner around such obstacles, but that requires not only looking up, but also judging the height of his partner in relation to the danger, a lot of work for a canine with many other things on his mind.

If the dog runs his trainer into the obstacle, the trainer will rework the scenario. They would stop, relocate the obstacle, and the trainer would tap on it, telling the dog, "NO." Then they would step back a few feet and approach the obstacle again, carefully. If the dog has learned the lesson, he will either guide the trainer around the obstacle, or he will stop and show the trainer that there is some form of danger. Through consistency, repetition and praise, the guide dog learns a skill unique to their profession.

While the training program is rigorous and carefully structured, the dogs still get the chance to be dogs - to rest, relax and play, in their off hours.

Guide Dogs of America prides itself on its kennel program, which begins servicing the dogs even before they come in for formal training. Each dog starts with a day-stay visit to the kennel, and works up to an overnight stay, and then an extended stay before they are brought in to begin formal training.

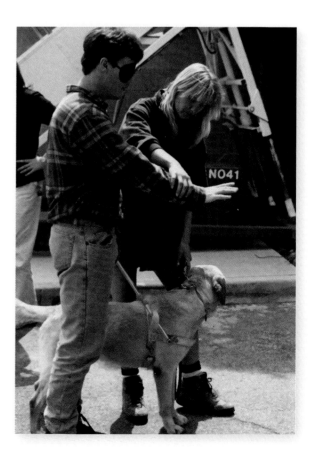

That allows the dog to get used to the environment and to bond with the kennel technicians who will care for them during their training program.

Each day, the dogs are given playtime and the chance to relax in the immaculately maintained, climate controlled kennel. Their progress is charted on a color coded board that tracks what medications they take and when, how often they eat, and how much they eat. In a typical year, Guide Dogs of America feeds more than 63,000 pounds of food to its furry boarders.

When the distinctive guide dog harness, invented by Captain L. A. Kreimer, the first trainer for Guide Dogs of America, is put on the dog, playtime is over and it's back to work to try to become the canine part of a guide dog team. ●

Chapter 16
Students

While the potential guide dogs are going through their intense training program, the Admissions office of GDA is screening applications from their future human partners.

Guide Dogs of America welcomes applications from people who are at least eighteen years of age, physically active, and have been declared legally blind by their doctor or ophthalmologist. There is no upper limit on age, and prospective students are required to have any health issues, such as diabetes, under control.

If a student is admitted to the program, the guide dog and the cost of their twenty-eight day training program at the Sylmar, California campus are free of charge.

Each application is reviewed by the Manager of Admissions and Graduate Services, who then contacts the potential student to answer any questions they may have about the school and to discuss the next steps in the application process.

Prospective students must demonstrate orientation and mobility skills, such as using a cane to identify objects and navigate around them.

Applicants are asked to provide personal references, and each reference is contacted by GDA staff. If those prove satisfactory the next step if the student evaluation process.

The Manager of Admissions and Graduate Services, the Director of Programs, and several of the professional train-ers will review the applicant's file and will then schedule an in-person interview if the applicant is local or they will ask them to submit a video if traveling to Sylmar is impractical.

The evaluation process begins the all important mission of matching the student with the right dog for their situation. Factors considered include whether the student lives in an urban, suburban or rural area; the level of activity in their normal day; the speed at which they walk; the composition of their household – are there children, other pets – and the modes of transportation they use most often.

Finally, when the application, review and evaluation processes are completed comes what school personnel call "The Magic of the Match," finding *exactly* the right canine partner for the student.

It usually takes from two to six months from the time of the initial application until a student is notified that they have been accepted and is invited to join a class at Sylmar. It can take longer depending on the needs of the student and whether the dogs currently in the program match their needs. The wait can be frustrating for students, but the reward of being matched with the perfect canine partner, one who will be at their side for every move for the next ten or more years, makes it all worthwhile.   ●

Rhonda Bissell

The Guide Dogs of America Partners in Trust program is overseen by Rhonda Bissell, Executive Assistant to the President of GDA, who has been with the organization for more than two decades.

Rhonda grew up on a farm in Michigan where she was surrounded by dogs and was fascinated at how they related to humans. She wrote several of her school papers on service animals and has had a lifelong admiration for the love and loyalty that dogs offer.

It was that fascination that led her to Guide Dogs of America where she began her career in the Admissions Department, then became Coordinator of the Volunteer Program, was assigned to speak on behalf of the organization, and helped establish the "751 Program" at Boeing in Seattle, where members of IAMAW Local 751 donate seven dollars and fifty-one cents from each paycheck to Guide Dogs of America through a payroll deduction.

She's also a volunteer puppy raiser, and says one of her biggest thrills is seeing a dog that she and her husband raised graduate the program and leave the school as a guide dog.

As director of the Wills and Trusts Department, Rhonda has seen donations ranging from a few hundred dollars to gifts in excess of one million dollars.

"It's touching to see the pride and satisfaction people get when they make their bequest," Bissell said, "they know that their legacy will live on in the form of the gift of sight for someone who will regain their freedom of mobility with a guide dog."

She's particularly proud of the time she spent in the school's "Under Blindfold" program, where instructors or staff members go through the student's training program while wearing a blindfold twenty-four hours a day.

"That really helped me understand what the students are going through," Bissell recalled, "something as simple as sitting in the lobby and hearing the door open and close. You have no idea if the person is still standing there, or if they passed through. It taught me to always identify myself when I enter a place where someone is visually impaired."

She also recalled being grateful for the gift of a talking watch. "With the blindfold on, you have no idea of whether its night or day. A friend gave me a talking watch – you press a button and it tells you what time it is. I loved that thing. I was always the first one up in the morning and I made the coffee. We had someone who was sighted place raised dots on the start button so I could get it working, and I learned to use my finger feel the water level as I filled the pot. You use your finger when you're pouring it too, but you're pouring hot coffee. After you burn your finger the first time, you learn to place it there very lightly after that."

"I know it's somewhat ironic to say, Bissell concluded, "but being under blindfold for nine days was an eye opening experience for me."

Chapter 17
On-Site Training

Students are brought to the Sylmar campus for a four week training session to learn how to navigate in the world with their guide dog partner.

They begin with what is known as Juno work – instruction and practice in obedience and guide dog handling techniques.

This includes voice commands, hand gestures, footwork, body movement while following the dog, making turns with the dog, and handling the leash for control.

Since it would be difficult for the student to master these skills with an actual dog, the trainers play the role of canine, which has the added benefit of providing the opportunity for verbal communication.

Instructors also provide a series of lectures on the theories involved in training and working with a guide dog to help the student develop a context for what they're about to learn.

Once the student has satisfactorily demonstrated the Juno work skills, it's time for them to be matched with their future guide dog. Great care is given to this match, with special attention given to the student's personality, size, energy level and pace. Information given during the application process about the student's lifestyle – where they live, how many people are in their household, how much traveling they do, and other elements of their home environment are carefully considered in choosing the right dog for them.

Once the student and guide dog are introduced to each other, they will be together constantly for the remainder of their time at the school.

Their training together begins with traveling on a route that is simple for both the dog and the student. Instructors choose sidewalks that are relatively smooth, wide, and free of obstacles and pedestrians. As the student and guide dog begin to feel their way

along the route, they will be receiving close supervision from their instructor, who supports and controls the dog until the student is able to do so on their own.

The second week of training brings more travel with the guide dog, this time on a route that offers more opportunity for variation. The routes are designed to allow each team to encounter increasingly difficult obstacles, street crossings and pedestrian traffic.

As the student becomes more comfortable working with the guide dog, instructors begin to allow more distance between themselves and the teams they are working with, but will remain in visual contact with them at all times.

Eventually, the student will demonstrate that they have memorized a basic route and are able to successfully complete the route without assistance or interference from the instructor.

With those skills mastered, the concept of intelligent disobedience is introduced – the guide dog will ignore commands that would place the student in harm's way – along with basic traffic training.

As the student and their new guide dog work, instructors are watching them carefully to evaluate their confidence, grasp of the basics, and their problem solving skills.

By the beginning of their third week of training, the team is ready to tackle more complex situations.

Instructors will take the students and their guide dogs to public buildings, indoor malls and shopping centers, college campuses, public parks, and other places with meandering paths and sidewalks. The student and their guide dog will ride city busses, trains and subways. They'll be worked in country settings where there are no sidewalks, and they'll be exposed to elevators, escalators and revolving doors. They'll also be brought to more challenging urban environments

where there are crowded sidewalks, busy streets, wide intersections, and lots of distractions.

Week four of training is a careful review to see that each student has mastered the skills necessary to work with a guide dog.

Instructors will be evaluating their ability to satisfactorily care and maintain their guide dog, their skill at working their guide dog independently along a basic route with no help from an instructor, and their basic rapport with their canine partner. Students will be expected to show satisfactory control of their guide dog, to demonstrate the mental and

physical ability to work with the guide dog, solve problems independently, and most importantly, to demonstrate that they can do all this with self confidence.

Graduation comes after the twenty-first day of training, and students who are getting their first guide dog remain at the school for a final week of fine tuning of their skills.

The real development begins when the student and their guide dog leave the Sylmar campus to begin their life together – a true partnership that will continue throughout their lives. ●

1431 Truman

Addax Tactical Inc.

Abba Pure

KSE Photography

For Lease Information Call
Gustavo (818) 270-9090

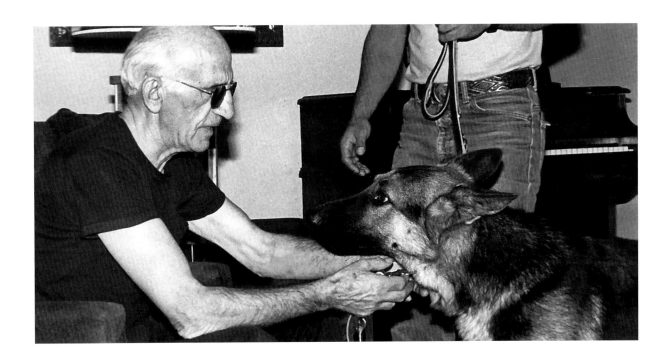

The Magic of the Match: Students eagerly await the moment they first meet their future guide dog.

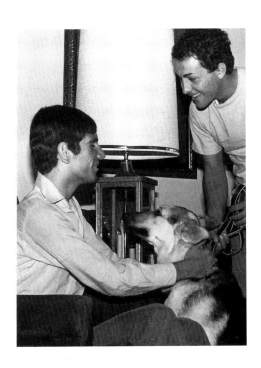

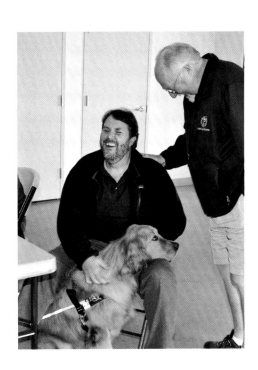

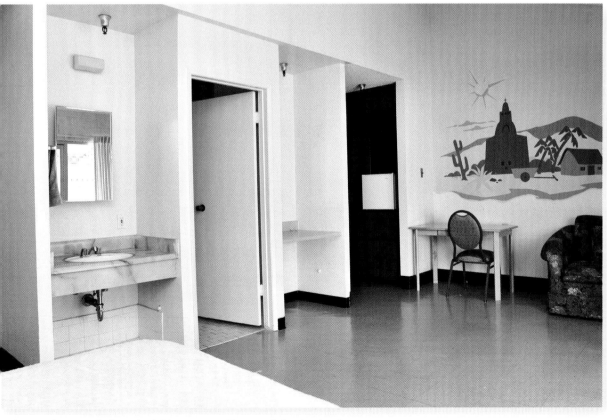

Students spend twenty-eight days at GDA's Sylmar campus. Above, a typical student dormitory room.

Chapter 18

A Student's Perspective

By Lorri Bernson, Guide Dogs of America Graduate

My Furry Eyes…

It wasn't going to happen to me. I was in the prime of my life with a great job, living my life as I wanted to… but it did. At age thirty-three, due to complications from diabetes, I lost all vision in my right eye and 95% in my left eye – and was told it could diminish even further – which it has. Knowing that diabetes is one of the leading causes of blindness, I still was never prepared for this. No one is. I was scared not knowing how my life would be; how would I pursue my dreams? How would I ever be happy again? Who would want to marry me? How would I be able to function independently, not only in the safety of my home, but outside in the world? Now, even a simple task such as pouring hot water into a cup was dangerous.

For many months and through several surgeries, I was on a roller coaster of having some vision to having none at all. It put me on the top of a fence and I had no idea which side I would land on: the sighted side or the blind side? My case became too tough even for some of the doctors who, in turn sent me across the country to those they thought could help. I had to stir up the strength to keep fighting to not let this complication of diabetes win. And I was not the only one affected. Blindness affects the whole family. To experience the demise of my vision and not be able to do anything about it was quite difficult, especially for a parent. There was nothing my mom could do except be there for me, share her strength, and somehow help me by leading the way to help make the necessary decisions – would I go for that one more surgery that might take all of my vision away in hopes that the opposite would happen? The pain of watching a family member go through any ordeal is heartbreaking.

When it was final that nothing else could be done to save my vision, I kept my chin up and at-

tempted to let denial take its course. I realized that I needed more help than I could give myself, or that I even wanted to admit. I got into a routine of listening to audio books and being "fine" with a life of just that….but only for so long. I needed more. Could a guide dog help me with this next step?

It took me a while to actually take to the idea of having a guide dog – mainly because one of the prerequisites was that I needed to learn how to use a white cane – one of the biggest hurdles for someone who is blind as that is an actual step toward accepting that this is what you are – blind. And now, everyone else would know it. I couldn't see myself walking in my neighborhood using the cane, because then… people would see me as a blind person and I wasn't sure I was ready for that to be so public. But then I realized it was a means to an end, that a guide dog would be the prize I could get if I just accepted what I had to do. So it not only helped me immensely, but it also told others that I was not going to move out of their way; rather they needed to work around my path. And it minimized the explaining of why I would need some assistance in certain situations.

When you lose your vision, you lose your self confidence, your mobility and most of all, your independence; it's the nature of the beast. I now had to rely on others to get me from point A to B safely which I did for several years. So I covered it up by always being out with another person who made it "look ok." Everything seemed "ok" until the day I was walking out of a restaurant and someone said to me "Oh, nice liquid lunch!" because I was walking unsteadily due to my blindness with a lot of objects in the way – not because I was drunk as the woman had concluded. That was when I knew I had to do something. Learning how to go about gaining a life of full

mobility back is where my story and the beginning of my very happy world begins...because, again... I wanted more.

Obtaining a Guide Dog:

When I started calling some of the different guide dog schools, I found that the programs were quite similar in their training. The emotional bond and family-like comfort that I felt when I visited Guide Dogs of America confirmed it was the school for me. I felt that the smaller class size would be a fit for me – with only ten students per class – I felt that I would get the personalized training that I was seeking. Also, with a smaller school, I learned then that GDA would spend a bit more time actually trying to match a student with the type of dog that would work best for the handler. When the trainers came to visit me for an interview, it was comforting to know that they were trying to get to know me in order to be able to make sure they had a dog that would fit into my life and that my life would be a world in which the dog would be happy. So I filled out the application, which included a medical report from my physician, a report from my ophthalmologist, and a list of references. Then I waited to hear the news. I was accepted into the program!

The letter came and I was full of excitement, nerves, and fear. I felt excitement knowing my life was going to change, nervous about how I was really going to do this, and fear of the unknown. Now I just had to wait for the right dog to come along. I received notice that they had an opening in an upcoming class. So, as class got closer and I knew I was in I started having dreams of what my dog would look like and constant thoughts of how we would work together and how this whole "guide dog thing" works.

Class:

The first day of my 28-day class was at hand! Not only was I going to live with a new dog, but at the same time, live in a dorm-like setting with nine other visually impaired people all from different walks of life. We all had one thing in common: we wanted a guide dog to enhance our world with independence. That goal kept us connected and supporting one another. Three days after we arrived at GDA for class, we were to receive our dogs, specifically selected for us. The only information the trainers told me that afternoon was my dog's name and breed. I heard: "….and he is a Golden Retriever named Nigel". At that point I lost it. I was overwhelmed with excitement by this point. They had a dog for me – *specifically for me*! We were then told to go into our rooms and wait for one of the trainers to bring our dog to us. The anticipation was heightened to the point where it was almost unbearable. Each time I heard a leash clanging and the nails of a dog walking down the long tile corridor I thought for sure it was coming to my room. And then it happened. The trainer knocked on my door. They came in, and my tears began a continuous flow. The most beautiful 78-pound, dark red dog came into my room. This was the furry partner that I was going to be responsible for taking care of while he in turn took care of me. He seemed almost human! We were left to ourselves for quite some time to get to know one another and start the ever so important bond that would take us more places than I ever imagined. Nigel walked in with confidence and such stature that I hoped I could match up to that. And then, the next day we went on our first walk together.

The first route was to be very basic, starting with the "Forward" command. I was so unsure of what to expect, having never walked with a guide dog. I picked up Nigel's harness handle and gave him that magical command: "Nigel, forward." I knew from that moment on, my safety was not only for me to provide, but that this amazing creature was going to lead the way. I thought we were going at a very fast pace, which is a common feeling when first walking with a guide dog, when in actuality, we were going very close to my natural pace. When Nigel automati-

cally stopped at the corner curb, it was so exhilarating. I knew that he was trained to do that, but to actually experience it was like nothing else. We were no longer on just a route; we were on the beginning of a path of adventure from here on in. As my confidence started to build, and the more I worked with him, the more I started to let go and start to trust. One of the most difficult things for a blind person is to learn how to trust a dog. This can sometimes take up to a year before you really have complete faith in your dog. Experiencing the dog actually doing his job over and over is what solidifies that trust.

As class went on and the training became more extensive, it tested my partnership with Nigel and more. Like two dance partners learning a new dance together we had frustrations, "a-ha" moments, and finally the thrill of knowing that if I really wanted to do something, I could do it. The schedule in class was tough. We worked six days a week, starting at 6:00am and ending after our dogs' last relieving time at 8:30pm. When the trainers raised the level of our independence, by backing off from being very close to us to putting an ever larger distance between us,

it was frightening. We ventured out to all types of areas and conditions in the community. We rode busses, walked on sidewalks and shopped in stores. Nigel was the perfect guide, and after going someplace only one time, he had a way of remembering it the next time we went in that direction, no matter how much time had passed since we'd been there.

GRADUATION:

Graduation day finally arrived: the day our class would present our new partnerships to the world as official graduated guide dog teams. At the same time, we'd witness our dogs' reactions to seeing their puppy raisers for the first time in several months. One hour before graduation, the raisers were welcomed into our individual rooms. I was nervous and tentative, not knowing how Nigel would react. Would he go to them and not want to be with me? Would they "approve" of me, the one who was matched with the dog they loved and had raised for almost two years? When they walked in, Nigel was on a leash and he immediately recognized them and went crazy with excitement. These dogs do not for-

get their puppy raisers, regardless of the time passed since their last meeting. He ran to them and then back to me, and repeated the sequence over and over. But what was most amazing was that after all of this, he came and stayed with me. It was a true example of one of the full circles that life brings.

At the ceremony, with hundreds of people in attendance, each graduate spoke of his or her feelings and adventures. The puppy raiser also spoke about the dog who had lived with them for eighteen months prior to formal training. It was quite an emotional day, filled with pride and contentment.

Life with a Guide Dog:

After a few more days of fine-tuning, it was time to leave the comfort and safety of the Guide Dogs of America Sylmar campus…to take what we learned and to go experience our new lives with our guide dogs at our sides. I was a bit tentative, knowing that the trainers would no longer be within physical range if needed. Nigel and I were now on our own. As we ventured into our new lives together, I realized so many things. I was now able to listen to the sounds of the life around me; rather than for sounds of danger in my path, as Nigel would take care of that. I was able to walk tall again with confidence, knowing that he and I would face any problem together, I was no longer alone. I found that having a guide dog was now my bridge to communicating with the public, who had largely ignored me when I was maneuvering with my cane. Standing on a corner with a cane, I would hear people around me, but no one would say anything to me, not even a "Good morning." Without eye contact, many people in the sighted world don't know how to communicate with someone who is blind. But that all changed. I now had a gorgeous dog next to me that was my "bridge." Almost everyone we passed by was now greeting me with "What a beautiful dog," which then led to conversations. We knew no strangers. I was now proud to be out with this wonderful partner at my side, fig-

uring things out together. To be able to just pick up and go when I wanted to, rather than having to wait to fit into someone else's schedule, was so empowering. I found myself transforming back into someone with confidence, drive, and motivation to keep going. We went to events to raise awareness of what having a guide dog can do; what an incredible gift I was given at a time that I needed it the most. My blindness was no longer about something that I lost, but rather something that I gained.

Retirement:

For a guide dog user, one of the most difficult decisions is when to retire a guide dog from his or her working duties. After eight and a half years together, Nigel was ten years old and had begun to show signs that the time was approaching to hang up his harness. As I prepared for Nigel's retirement, I had to think about what life will be like without Nigel at my side.

Nigel had been not only my eyes, but my heart and my best friend, constantly at my side. He had become every much a part of me as my hands or my legs. When I received Nigel, never in my life did my thoughts ever lead me to believe that my life would be so full, independent and happy.

But Nigel was slowing down and, as much as I didn't want to think about the fact that his retirement time was nearing…I had to.

I was determined that Nigel would spend his retirement with me. I knew it would be an enormous and emotional transition for both of us, but I reluctantly started the process and began leaving Nigel home more often so he and I could get used to not being with one another 24/7…this was the tough part. Then the time came when there was a match for me, and a new dog was coming into our lives. I wondered how Nigel would feel when I left the house with another dog. Would he feel left behind or would he be happy to go back to bed with the house quiet and all to himself? The trainers say that dogs adjust quickly, but my love for Nigel made the process a difficult one.

The experience of making the transition from your first dog to your second is referred to as "second dog syndrome." I knew my second dog would be a totally different dog from Nigel and could not be expected to just step in and act like a seasoned dog, but comparisons were inevitable. I had to remind myself that it took Nigel and me some time to become the team that we were, and I needed to give my next dog that time as well.

They say that your first guide dog is the one you always remember the most – the one that "changed your life." I will always carry with me the love, companionship and unimaginable bond that Nigel and I have.

The idea of not having Nigel next to me all the time broke my heart, but what mended it was knowing that the path we started on together could continue with another blessing by my side.

I submitted my application to Guide Dogs of America for a successor to Nigel – because while someone else would be doing his job, no dog would ever *replace* him. While I was waiting to hear that they had found another dog for me, a puppy raiser asked me, "Is it time to pass the torch?" Actually, there is no torch to pass – as that light will burn forever; a new torch will be lit with many new paths to conquer with my next guide dog. It will just be a different light shining the way for me, but with equal brightness.

Preparing for a new Guide Dog:

I thought that deciding it was time to retire Nigel was one of the most difficult things I have ever had to do, until I realized I wasn't able to keep him – that was worse. Nigel stayed with friends of mine for a few weeks while I attended class to receive my second guide dog, "Carter." When Nigel returned to me, I knew within minutes that I couldn't physically and emotionally have both Carter and Nigel. It was great to see the two of them play together, yet at the same time I realized that I felt very disconnected from both

of them. Everything I was fearful of regarding having two dogs was coming into the forefront of my mind instead of in the back of my mind where I could keep it quiet. Taking care of two big dogs alone in an apartment would be tough. Who would watch Nigel when I was out with Carter? What if Nigel needed me and I wasn't with him? What if Carter and I didn't bond as expected as a result of still having Nigel with me? Within these minutes, I thought about how I went back to GDA to receive another guide dog so that I could continue growing. If I would always be worried about Nigel at home, then my growth, and congruently, my relationship with Carter, would suffer. It took only a few minutes with all three of us together before I came to the devastating conclusion that Nigel could not stay with me. My first call was to Nigel's puppy raisers who had always expressed that if there ever came a time I could not have him, their home would once again be his. That same afternoon, they picked him up, and with all the mutual love they had for each other, he went to live where he grew up. It was an incredibly tough day in my life, yet another example of the full circle that happens in life. I now see Nigel as often as possible, and he holds the most sacred part of my heart, as a first love tends to do. He remains connected to me, but the bond is now back with his puppy raisers, as it should be.

And now there's Carter...a remarkably handsome Golden Retriever/Labrador Retriever cross who is full of spirit and love and whose goal in life is to bring a smile to the faces of all who meet him as he guides me on my path as Nigel did. The day I received Carter in class I was filled with so many different thoughts and emotions. I was sad as it really marked the "ending" of Nigel and me as a team. It was over and now I had to start out again, hoping that "second dog syndrome" would not take its toll too harshly. But, when Carter came into my room, as Nigel did eight years prior, almost to the day, I started to feel lifted. Here was this big, gorgeous, loving, silly dog that wiggled all around me.

Lorri Bernson with "Carter" (left) and "Nigel" (right).

As the days went by in class, just as in my first class, there were trepidation and emotions; this dog was not Nigel. He walked more "bouncy", I needed to handle him differently, my tone of voice needed to be a little different – all things expected because it was something I wasn't used to. And soon, Carter taught me that I could love again, and that the road ahead is for us to travel together…enjoying the fact that we would be safe together. His personality is infectious, and to walk beside him fills my heart.

Carter and I continue to have very few limitations as to what we can do and where we can go. We have traveled on cruises and airplanes, hoping to spread the word to others, just by watching us, that having a guide dog can change the life of someone who is blind. Many of the students at Guide Dogs of America and their canine partners are sponsored by a charitable group or an individual who contribute the money to cover the cost of our dog and our training. Carter and I were very fortunate to be sponsored by the Los Angeles Dodger's Dream Foundation, and Ned Colletti, General Manager of the team. That connection resulted in an invitation for me to throw out the first pitch at a Dodger's home game, with Carter right by my side. With thousands of

fans watching from the stands, and who knows how many watching on television, I took a moment before I threw my pitch from the mound to consider how blessed I really am. Sometimes life can throw you a curveball, but the important thing is that you stay in the game and keep pitching.

My life has been forever changed for the better, thanks to two sets of "furry eyes," and the wonderful people at Guide Dogs of America. ●

PART III

Support for Guide Dogs Of America

"Guide Dogs of America captures the very spirit of trade union solidarity: where we look out for our own and do everything we possibly can to help those in society who are less fortunate."

(R. Thomas Buffenbarger, IAM International President)

Chapter 19

The I.A.M. – There From the Beginning

Perhaps the most important meeting of Joseph Jones' very eventful life is the one he attended on October 1, 1946. It was on that day that he made a presentation to the Executive Council of the International Association of Machinists, the union he had been a member of since 1902.

He sat at the long conference table at their Washington, D.C., headquarters unable to see their faces, but ultimately able to determine what was in their hearts. He outlined his concept of an organization that would provide scientifically trained guide dogs to the visually impaired, and his program would differ from other programs already doing that in two critical respects: there would be no age limitations on who could receive a dog; and more importantly, these dogs would be provided free of charge.

The men of the Executive Council, older, from factory shop floors and railroad yards, and hardened through years of making their ways up through the ranks of one of the largest labor unions in the United States and Canada, listened intently to the plea of their brother, and voted unanimously to commit the power of the union to his cause.

They could have given him a check from their treasury, wished him well, and sent him on his way. That is how many other organizations would have handled the situation. Instead, they did something profoundly more important: they endorsed his idea and made it clear to their membership, which was approaching a million people, that this was a cause worthy of their support.

The members of the IAM responded immediately and generously. Donations from individual members, local lodges, districts and territories began to flow in immediately. Fundraising events were held, and thousands of members and their families across the United States and Canada attended. Jones' organization was given significant publicity in the union's monthly journal and weekly newspaper, and Jones was invited to address the delegates at each future IAM convention.

Jones had the power of his union behind him, and the IAM had officially adopted a signature charity.

That relationship has endured to this day.

There are many ways the members of the International Association of Machinists and Aerospace Workers have carried out the wishes expressed at that fateful meeting in 1946.

The Annual William W. Winpisinger Charity Banquet

Every year since 1980, Guide Dogs of America holds a banquet in Las Vegas, Nevada to honor the memory of William W. Winpisinger who, as President of the IAMAW, was vitally important to revitalizing the program when it was in dire straits financially.

Winpisinger arranged to have the IAM buy the mortgage on the newly constructed Sylmar campus, allowing Guide Dogs of America to pay the loan back interest-free. He also provided emergency funding to keep the organization afloat when economic conditions threatened its very survival. Winpisinger had a deep personal commitment to seeing GDA succeed, and recruited some of his best

Gift of Sight recipient Kevin Kelly (right) is joined by his very dapper family, sons Joe, Billy and John, and wife Patricia, at the Winpisinger Dinner in Las Vegas.

managers from within the union to put the organization back on track.

The first banquet in his honor was held at Caesar's Palace in 1980. Bud Melvin, who was then President of International Guiding Eyes, handled every detail himself, and encouraged people to buy tickets, but not to come to the dinner – because if they came he had to feed them, and that cost money – every ticket sold to someone who did not attend was pure profit.

From those humble beginnings, with the support of the IAMAW, several generous corporate sponsors, and continuing support from individuals and organizations, the Winpisinger Banquet, which has expanded to include a charity golf tournament and a motorcycle ride, now raises more than a million dollars each year.

Guide Dogs of America Booths at IAMAW Events

Any time the IAMAW holds a large event, from their quadrennial Grand Lodge Convention to legislative conferences, territorial conferences, international staff conferences or any other large gathering, Guide Dogs of America is given a prominent place to display their program and solicit support.

Members have responded generously, and the chance to see guide dogs in action has always been a big draw. The pride of IAM members in their signature charity is evidenced by their eagerness to dig into their own pockets to do their bit to help sustain GDA.

Hawgs for Dogs Motorcycle Charity Ride and Annual Harley Davidson Raffle

Harley Davidson motorcycles, those iconic American machines, are made by members of the IAM. The union has many motorcycle enthusiasts, and each year since 1990, a growing number of those bikers have held a charity ride they call "Hawgs for Dogs." The first one raised about what it cost to train one guide dog team at the time, but today the event raises many times that amount.

IAM Fundraising Events for Guide Dogs of America

It would be almost impossible to list every type of charity event held on behalf of Guide Dogs of America by the various elements of the IAMAW. One wag said: "If it's legal, we've probably done it."

Beginning with a variety show held in 1947, by District 15 in New York City, which was followed by an even bigger variety show in Hollywood a year later sponsored by the District and Local Lodges of Southern California, the IAM has had an ongoing friendly competition to see which group can be the most creative and raise the most money.

Territories, Districts, and Local Lodges have sponsored car shows, GDA nights at professional baseball games, trap shooting contests, fishing derbies, cigar parties, lobster feeds, golf tournaments, and all other manners of fundraisers. The pride and spirit of IAM members in their support for Guide Dogs of America is a true display of how to put the "fun" in "fundraising." ●

IAM General Vice President Phil Gruber (left), General Secretary Treasurer Warren Mart (second from right) and International President Tom Buffenbarger (right) take aim during a trap shooting contest.

Chapter 20
Corporate Partners

Guide Dogs of America has enjoyed the generous support of a number of corporate partners over the years.

The Lockheed Corporation was among the first to participate, with its "Buck of the Month Club," which began contributing to International Guiding Eyes in 1948. Formed as a partnership between the company and its employees (many of whom were IAM members), the Buck of the Month Club allowed employees to have twenty-five cents per week deducted from their paychecks and aggregated into a fund to support worthwhile charities.

Encouraged by that association with International Guiding Eyes, Lockheed has remained committed to the organization over the years, demonstrating their support by matching employee's contributions and making other significant donations to Guide Dogs of America.

Boeing Corporation cooperates with IAMAW Local 751 in Seattle to coordinate the "751 Club," where members have seven dollars and fifty-one cents deducted from each paycheck and sent directly to Guide Dogs of America.

Other large corporations have also provided assistance through matching employee contributions, donating equipment, sponsoring charity events, and providing in-kind contributions.

Among the many corporations to demonstrate their support are Harley Davidson, UPS, and the United States Sugar Corporation.   ●

Chapter 21
Two Special Families

Paul Morton

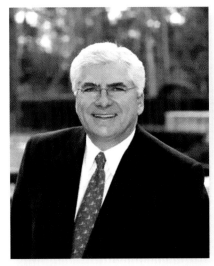

J. Weldon Granger

Among the many individuals and organizations that have supported Guide Dogs of America, two in particular stand out for their multi-generational generosity.

The Grangers and the Mortons have become a true part of the Guide Dogs of America family through their ongoing contributions and support.

The Grangers

J. Weldon Granger, a Houston attorney, was born in Erath, Louisiana. He attended the University of Southwestern Louisiana, and received his law degree from the South Texas College of Law.

Granger founded Jones Granger, a national law firm specializing in federal litigation and representation of members of the railway labor industry.

His other business interests include real estate development and thoroughbred horse breeding, and he is a major patron of the arts.

He met William Winpisinger, then President of the IAM, through his legal profession, and the two became friends. Before long, Winpisinger convinced Granger to become involved with International Guiding Eyes, and for Granger, it was love at first sight.

"My father was blind in one eye," Granger recalled, and as a young man I often thought about what it would be like to be blinded in both eyes."

Granger's love of animals, desire to support causes important to the IAM, and his sensitivity to the plight of the visually impaired made participating with Guide Dogs "an easy sell."

In 1992, when Texas Agriculture and Mining University developed a pilot program to attempt to breed hip dysplasia out of guide dog lines, IGE President Bud Melvin asked Weldon Granger to help. Texas A&M was particularly interested in having IGE participate because they had thorough records of their breed lines covering the past forty years. The university needed a substantial amount of money to embark on the project, and Weldon Granger donated a quarter of a million dollars to make it possible.

Granger was proud to help a worthwhile cause, and when Bud Melvin asked him if he would like anything in return, Granger said that the satisfaction of giving a gift that could possibly help thousands of people was quite enough. He did suggest that if IGE had any career change dogs available, he'd like to adopt one.

Melvin responded by sending the next available puppy, a German Shepherd named "Boomer," to Houston to live with Weldon Granger, his wife Fran, and their children Jennifer, John and Jason.

Boomer quickly became a member of the family, one the Granger kids jokingly nicknamed "the two hundred and fifty thousand dollar dog," a riff on a popular television show of the time called "The Six Million Dollar Man."

Weldon Granger continued to support Guide Dogs of America and brought his children along to the many GDA events he attended.

"I was honored to receive the 'Gift of Sight Award' at the Winpisinger Banquet in 1993," Granger recalled. "My parents were there, along with my wife Fran and our children. Jason was seven years old then, and fell asleep in his chair. Now he's in his thirties, runs his own business, and contributes to Guide Dogs of America."

Jason's company, Employee Benefit Systems, is a proud supporter of GDA, and along with his brother John's Graystone Consulting, helps sponsor the annual Winpisinger Charity Golf Tournament.

"I'm proud of the mission and growth of Guide Dogs of America," Granger said, "my family truly believes in this organization, and it's something we're going to continue to support."

The Mortons

Tom Morton grew up in San Mateo, California, and graduated from Stanford University. He started out by developing a successful meat business, but soon decided that if he wanted to put his six children through college, he'd have to switch careers, and in 1969, he started his own investment firm, specializing in retirement planning for people in the automotive and entertainment industries. His mantra was one of providing "retirement with dignity," to workers who might not otherwise be familiar with the world of investing.

One of his clients was the local lodge where Frank Souza, a Winpisinger confidante was a leader, and before long Souza recruited Tom Morton to become active in supporting Guide Dogs of America.

"There wasn't a lot of fluff," Tom Morton's son Paul recalled. "It was just: 'This is a good thing, you've got to get involved.' If it was a golf ball, a kid or a dog, you had a pretty good chance of getting his support. If it was a combination of those two or three things, you were a cinch."

At Souza's urging, Tom Morton became a major sponsor for a Guide Dogs of America golf tournament in the Northern California Bay Area.

Morton looked into the organization he was sponsoring and one of the things that attracted his

Tom and Helen K. Morton: Helen has remained a steadfast supporter of GDA.

Jason, Weldon and John Granger: "My family truly believes in this organization," Weldon said.

attention was the program of allowing people to adopt "career change" dogs, those that for whatever reason were not suitable for guide dog work. He soon was given a Golden Retriever puppy they named "Sweeps," because his tail never stood still and he could sweep anything off a table in the blink of an eye.

Recalling his father's love for the adopted dog, Paul Morton said, "Sweeps dragged him whatever rest of the way there was into the support structure that is Guide Dogs. He ended up going to graduations, visiting the campus, and became thoroughly enthralled with Guide Dogs and then really infused that love into all of us."

"When my father passed away," Paul Morton continued, "one of the things he asked of us was that we continue to be involved with Guide Dogs of America. He had been on the board of directors, and I was asked to take his place, and was pleased to do so. My step-mother is still an ardent supporter of the cause, and we continue to be involved in various ways."

Paul Morton also inherited his father's fondness for dogs.

"I guess the dog bug was part of my marriage criteria," he said, "because I married a woman whose dad was equally crazy about dogs, and now we have five dogs, three of whom are rescues."

Recalling a recent graduation ceremony he attended, Paul Morton said he still gets goose bumps thinking about what he witnessed.

"It's amazing to me that what these folks have in common is not their being sight impaired. What they have in common is this amazing desire to be independent. And they work so incredibly hard to achieve that – the humans and their partner dogs. It's a reminder of how blessed we are, those of us who sometimes take for granted the ability to see, and to function independently without thinking about it. And then you watch folks from all different walks of

Tom Morton and "Sweeps."

life - all with different stories - what they're striving for is to reclaim their independence. The work of Guide Dogs of America makes that happen."

Brian Morton, Paul's brother and the President of Mc Morgan and Company, is also an active supporter of GDA. Brian received the Gift of Sight Award in 2011 for his contributions, fundraising and support of the efforts of IAM District Lodge 190 to raise funds in the San Francisco Bay Area.

Paul Morton has involved his daughters, Emily and Jenny, in GDA activities, the beginning of a third generation of Morton family support.

"I take my two girls to the GDA open house," Morton said, "it's one of the great learning experiences I can provide to my kids and have them see what goes on and how people work hard to achieve some of the basic things in life."

For both the Granger and Morton families, support for Guide Dogs of America has been one of the ties that bind generations together. ●

Chapter 22
Hollywood Stars

Hollywood stars of screen, television, and radio have always been among Guide Dogs of America's biggest supporters.

It's a love affair that started with the extravagant charity benefit at Hollywood's Shrine Auditorium in 1948, and continues to this day.

Many of Hollywood's brightest stars have lent their time, talents and money to help provide guide dogs for the visually impaired.

John Wayne performed on a radio broadcast of Ralph Edward's popular show, "Truth or Consequences" featuring International Guiding Eyes in 1949, and posed proudly for a picture with IGE founder Joseph Jones, and head trainer Captain L.A. Kreimer.

Clark Gable and his wife Carole Lombard donated their stable to IGE, and the restored building stands today on the Sylmar campus, where it is still in use.

Donald O'Connor, an old school song and dance man famous for his movies with "Francis the Talking Mule," served as the celebrity master of ceremonies for the 1948 benefit, and was so impressed with the mission of IGE that he took a seat on the organization's board of directors.

Following his lead, such notables as Jonathan Winters, Zsa Zsa Gabor, and Lucille Ball have served on the IGE Board of Directors.

Actors Cliff Robertson, Ed Asner, Dudley Moore, and Amanda Righetti have each starred in a film or video to promote the organization.

Jackie Cooper, Roy Rodgers, and Gail Davis (better known as Annie Oakley), raised funds for IGE and attended many events at the North Hollywood facility of IGE.

Andy Griffith was the first Hollywood star to contribute the entire cost for fielding a guide dog team.

David Hasselhoff, Heather Thomas, and Paula Abdul have each posed for Guide Dogs of America fundraising posters, and Betty White has contributed her time and money to the organization for more than fifty years.

Scores of other Hollywood personalities have lent their support to Guide Dogs of America, a tradition that continues to this day.

Amanda Righetti, star of several movies and the popular CBS Television series "The Mentalist" is the latest of several generations of Hollywood stars to lend their voice and talents to Guide Dogs of America.

"It's a great cause to be involved with," Righetti said, "but it's also about giving back to your community. When you're in the business if having visibility within certain communities and nationally, I think it's important to be part of something that helps people."

"I'm really excited to know about this organization and what they're doing for the visually impaired. I think it's amazing that they front the costs for everything for the visually impaired to come here, and to have a dog and a companion that can help them get around. I wish more people would become involved." ●

(Left to right) Radio host Ralph Edwards, Captain L.A. Kreimer, guide dog recipient, actor John Wayne, Joseph W. Jones, Sr.

Cowboy star Roy Rogers.

Actress Debbie Reynolds.

Actress Cleo Moore with guide dog "Ruby."

Founder Joseph Jones with Donald O'Connor at the 1948 benefit.

Baseball legend Lefty O'Doul: many baseball teams sponsored charity nights to support guide dogs.

Actor Edd Byrnes, "Kookie" on 77 Sunset Strip, addresses graduates.

Actress June Allyson filmed a made-for-television movie at Guide Dogs of America.

Actor Gary Cooper was an active supporter of International Guiding Eyes.

Actor and comedian Jonathan Winters became an honorary Chairman of International Guiding Eyes, and did tireless fundraising for the school.

Actress Julie Adams.

Actors Jack Albertson (center, wearing hat) and Red Buttons (center, wearing necktie) join an International Guiding Eyes graduating class.

Actress Gail Davis, better known as "Annie Oakley," poses with IGE graduates.

Actress Nadja Posey with three graduates.

Actor George Lindsay, better known as "Goober," and actress Nancy Kulp, better known as "Miss Hathaway" at the IGE campus.

Actress Betty White (center wearing kerchief, and below left) has been a supporter of IGE and GDA for more than three decades.

Actress Cheryl McManus was a GDA celebrity spokesperson.

Actor Cliff Robertson.

Actor David Hasselhoff.

IAM President George Kourpias poses with actor Dudley Moore.

Chapter 23
Events for a Worthy Cause

In addition to vast array of fundraising activities of the IAM, Hollywood stars, and Guide Dogs of America's corporate partners, the organization has always hosted its own events.

The people of Southern California have flocked to the Guide Dogs of America campus to support such varied activities as dog shows, bicycle races, fashion shows, celebrity chili cook-offs, matchbox derby races, motorcycle runs, and even an Arabian horse show.

The annual open house, featuring an obstacle course for puppies in training and a silent auction, is always a popular draw because it affords people the opportunity to see the Sylmar facilities while relaxing and having fun.

One of the most sought-after raffle prizes is the opportunity to spend a day with a Guide Dogs of America trainer and to experience the sensation of a blindfold walk with a well trained Guide Dog providing effortless mobility through a world of darkness.

Guide Dogs of America is also a popular destination for church and school groups. Tours offer the opportunity to see the fruits of more than sixty years of people pulling together to fulfill Joseph W. Jones' dream of providing scientifically trained guide dogs free of charge to the visually impaired. ●

EYES FOR THE BLIND

PADRES VS STARS

GUIDING EYE DAY

benefit baseball game to provide guide dogs for the blind

sponsored by
MACHINISTS UNION DISTRICT 50

SAT. MAY 14

2:15 P.M.   LANE FIELD

TICKETS ON SALE HERE
also at
Machinists Union Hall
3911 Pacific Hwy., San Diego
Machinists Lodge 755
383 National, Chula Vista
or from your
UNION COMMITTEEMAN

52

U.S. Sugar President and CEO Bob Buker (right) joins golfers John Ciardi, Chuck Shide and Pat Halley.

International Association of Machinists and Aerospace Workers
9000 Machinists Place
Upper Marlboro, MD 20772

□□□

PAY to
the order of _____ Guide Dogs of America

Date Nov. 19, 20

$ 18,652.00

Eighteen Thousand and Six Hundred Fifty Two

For 2011 Contribution
IAM Calendar Sales

Dollars

⑈000000000⑈ 000000000⑈ 0000

Warren L. Mart

IAM President Tom Buffenbarger presents a check to Guide Dogs of America President Dale Hartford.

Brian Morton accepts a 2011 Gift of Sight Award from IAM President Tom Buffenbarger.

GDA President Dale Hartford and IAM President Tom Buffenbarger flank IAM General Vice President Robert Martinez, a 2011 Gift of Sight Award recipient.

Brian, Tom and Paul Morton.

Retired GDA President Jay Bormann.

International Association of Machinists and Aerospace Workers
9000 Machinists Place
Upper Marlboro, MD 20772

Date ___ 2005

PAY to the order of _____ Guide Dogs of America _____ $ 29,894.00

Twenty Nine Thousand and Eight Hundred Ninety Four Dollars

2005 Contribution
For ___ IAM Calendar Sales

PART IV

How You Can Help

"Guide Dogs of America depends on your generosity. We do not receive financial assistance from any level of government. Every dollar used to breed the puppies, train the young dogs, train the students, run the school and provide graduate services comes from donations."

(Dale Hartford, GDA President)

Chapter 24
How You Can Help

Joseph W. Jones, the founder of what is now known as Guide Dogs of America, had a dream: he wanted to provide scientifically trained guide dogs, free of charge, to the visually impaired.

Since its inception in 1948 as International Guiding Eyes, Incorporated, Guide Dogs of America has never charged its students for their dog or the cost of their month-long training stay at the school's facility.

Guide Dogs of America does not receive financial assistance from any level of the government. Every dollar used to breed the puppies, train the young dogs, train the students, run the school, and provide graduate services comes from donations.

Through the generosity of individuals, foundations, corporations and other organizations, Guide Dogs of America has been able to fulfill its mission of providing these loyal and loving dogs.

You can be a part of this worthwhile cause.

You can provide the support that will help Guide Dogs of America continue its legacy of providing the visually impaired with the dogs that will give them trust, companionship, love and freedom.

SPONSORSHIPS

Every dollar donated helps the cause. Guide Dogs of America invites you to become a partner via a range of sponsorship opportunities:

Puppy Sponsor

This type of sponsorship is the most popular with individuals and businesses that want to become involved on a more personal level, but do not have the time to devote to raising a puppy.

Your donation covers the cost of the basic puppy kit: leash, collar, identification tag, and bowl, ten to forty pounds of dog food, microchip, medical costs for spaying or neutering, vaccinations and veterinarian visits, periodic evaluations by training and puppy department staff, obedience training, puppy bib, and adult jacket.

As a sponsor you will receive photographs and a written update on a quarterly basis and your name will be embroidered on the puppy's jacket. Your puppy will be thoroughly evaluated at eighteen to twenty months of age to determine if it is eligible to continue on to formal guide dog training or be selected for our breeding program. Finally, if your dog successfully completes its training course, you will receive an invitation to our awards ceremony with special recognition for your generosity.

It is important to remember that not all of our puppies go on to be guide dogs. In fact, approximately forty percent are removed from the program due to problems with health or temperament, these can include allergies, hip dysplasia, overly friendly dogs, dogs distracted by cats or other canines, or other issues that would make it difficult for the dog to function at peak performance. These issues can arise even after the dog has entered the normal guide dog training program. While it is tremendously disappointing when a dog is removed from the program, the safety and well being of the students at Guide Dogs of America is always the primary concern.

If it is determined that your sponsored puppy is not suited for guide work, the puppy raiser is given the option of keeping it as a family pet. At that time, your sponsorship donation will be applied toward the next class graduating, and you will be acknowledged at their awards ceremony.

Newborn Puppy Sponsor

You will receive a certificate with a photo of a newborn puppy. Your gift covers the cost of breeding and delivery.

Sponsor A Litter of Puppies

You will receive a photo of the mother and her litter of puppies. Your donation covers the cost of breeding, delivery and all expenses for the puppies first seven weeks.

Student Accommodation Sponsor

Your gift covers the cost of room and board expenses for the student's twenty-eight day stay at the school in the student dormitory, travel expenses, and a guide dog graduation kit for one student.

Guide Dog Sponsor

Your donation covers all of the breeding, puppy and medical expenses plus all guide dog training. Guide Dog Sponsors have the opportunity to choose the breed of dog and are invited and acknowledged at graduation.

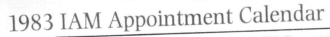

1983 IAM Appointment Calendar

A Salute to International Guiding Eyes from the union that cares

Student Sponsor

This covers the cost of transportation, room and board at GDA for the in-residence training period of twenty-eight days, training, activities and materials to train the student to use a guide dog. Student sponsors have the opportunity to choose which student they wish to sponsor and are invited and acknowledged at graduation.

Guide Dog Team Sponsor

This covers all of the above expenses. It allows you to sponsor the complete partnership, from breeding to graduation, of a dog and student. You will be invited and acknowledged at graduation for your extraordinary generosity.

GIVING OPPORTUNITIES

Donate Cash

A cash gift by check is one of the most common and easiest methods of making a charitable contribution.

If you itemize income tax deductions on your tax return, you can realize a deduction equal to the full value of your gift.

The annual limitation on the use of charitable deductions claimed for gifts to public charitable organizations is fifty percent of your adjusted gross income for cash gifts. Any unused deduction can be carried over for up to five additional years, giving you six full years to use the deduction.

To make a cash contribution, send a check payable to Guide Dogs of America to 13445 Glenoaks Boulevard, Sylmar, California 91342.

If you wish to have your contribution remain anonymous, please so indicate.

Gifts in Honor or in Memory

Celebrate important people, events or pets in your life by contributing to Guide Dogs of America. You may make the donation "in honor of," or "in memory of," a special person, an important occasion or a beloved pet.

Guide Dogs of America will send an acknowledgement card to the person you specify, which will show how much you care about your loved ones and the important work of Guide Dogs of America.

Fundraising Events

Enjoy yourself while supporting Guide Dogs of America by participating in any of the fun-filled events at the Sylmar campus, or those sponsored by the IAM throughout the United States and Canada.

Events at Sylmar include graduations, the annual Open House, and the motorcycle Ride for Guides.

Local Lodges of the International Association of Machinists sponsor a wide range of events throughout the year including golf tournaments, fishing derbies, car shows, lobster feeds, and trap shooting contests. To find an IAM event near you, consult the Guide Dogs of America website: guidedogsofamerica.org/events

Matching Gifts

Many employers will match the gifts their employees make to charitable organizations, doubling the impact of the gift. Ask your employer if they will be willing to offer this match.

Donate Stocks or Securities

One of the main benefits of giving stock is that you can provide a valuable gift and minimize your taxes. You will receive a tax deduction letter for your donation based on the average price of the security on the date you give the gift. You thereby avoid having to sell the security and pay taxes on the gain.

PARTNERS IN TRUST

Wills, Bequests and Trusts

Make a gift that will last a lifetime and beyond. By providing Life Income Gifts and Bequests, your donation continues working beyond your lifetime to help others enjoy increased mobility and independence with a loyal and loving guide dog partnership.

Charitable organizations such as Guide Dogs of America are not subject to gift or estate taxes, so your gift continues to support causes close to your heart without being diminished.

Guide Dogs of America acknowledges contributions of this nature by making you part of their Partners in Trust Society.

There are a number of creative ways you can participate in this worthwhile program:

Cash Bequest

You can designate that Guide Dogs of America receive a specified amount of cash from your estate.

Your Retirement Plan Assets

Assets remaining in retirement plans funded with pre-tax dollars are considered "income in respect of a decedent" at your death. So the amount left to heirs is diminished not only by estate taxes, but the recipient must also pay income taxes on it.

If you can make other provisions for your family, there is a better option for your retirement plan assets – a charitable gift after your lifetime.

To name Guide Dogs of America as your beneficiary, first consult your advisor, then instruct the plan administrator of your decision and sign whatever form is required. For an IRA or Keogh plan you administer personally, notify the custodian in writing and keep a copy with your valuable papers.

Life Insurance

A gift of your life insurance could be a sensible, as well as generous donation to Guide Dogs of America. If you make GDA the owner of the policy, you will normally receive an income tax deduction for the policy's fair market cost basis, if lower, on the date of the gift.

If you name Guide Dogs of America as the beneficiary of the policy (and retain ownership), you won't be eligible for current tax benefits because the gift is revocable at any time.

Whether you name Guide Dogs of America as owner of the policy or name us as the beneficiary while you retain ownership, your estate will not pay estate taxes on the policy proceeds received by Guide Dogs of America.

Retained Life Estate

A gift of your home, vacation home, condominium, ranch or farm, with the reservation of the right to use it for life, results in a charitable deduction on your income tax return.

You can continue to live in your residence for your lifetime, knowing that it will pass to Guide Dogs of America tax free.

Gift of Real Estate

You can avoid paying significant capital gains taxes on real estate such as commercial buildings or vacant land by donating it to Guide Dogs of America.

Your gift creates an enduring testimonial of your interest in our mission, and you may be eligible for valuable tax benefits.

Each donor making a bequest receives a special Partners in Trust gift, a beautiful crystal jar that makes an elegant addition to your desk, countertop or end table, whether you fill it with jelly beans or doggie bones.

OTHER OPPORTUNITIES TO HELP

There are many other ways, large and small, that you can become a member of the Guide Dogs of America community.

Check out the "How to Help" section of the Guide Dogs of America website: **guidedogsofamerica.org**

Among the many creative ways you can help Guide Dogs of America include donating airline frequent flier miles, purchasing GDA merchandise, and buying specific items on their wish list for students or dogs.

SPECIAL OPPORTUNITIES FOR RESIDENTS OF SOUTHERN CALIFORNIA

If you live within driving distance of Los Angeles, there are special ways you can help Guide Dogs of America:

Raise A Puppy

As a volunteer puppy raiser for GDA you will play an essential part in making sure your puppy receives the proper socialization needed to help adjust to the important job it will be doing later in life.

The puppy raiser is required to teach the puppy basic obedience, such as how to walk on a leash, how to sit, stay, lay down and come when called.

The puppy returns to Guide Dogs of America for formal training at about eighteen months of age. You'll be invited to a special "In For Training" luncheon, and any sadness at parting with your puppy will in time be overcome by the pride and joy of seeing it become the partner of a visually impaired student, allowing them to regain their independence.

To learn more about the puppy raising program, call Guide Dogs of America at (818) 362-5834 , or visit our website at guidedogsofamerica.org.

Donate Your Car or Vehicle

If you live in Southern California and have an unwanted car, truck, motorcycle, boat or recreational vehicle, in running condition or not, you may donate it to Guide Dogs of America and receive a tax deduction for the fair market value of the vehicle.

Volunteer Your Time

Guide Dogs of America welcomes volunteers who are at least eighteen years of age, offering a wide variety of opportunities, including clerical and general help, tour guides, speakers, and volunteers to help coordinate special events. ●

Notes

Chapter 1: The Guide Dog Movement

(1) *"The Voice of the Blind,"* by Captain L.A. Kreimer (1940) p 3

(2) *"Independent Vision, Dorothy Harrison Eustace and the Story of the Seeing Eye,"* by Miriam Ascarelli (Purdue University Press, 2010) p 37

(3) Saturday Evening Post: *"The Seeing Eye,"* by Dorothy Harrison Eustace, November 7, 1927, p 43

(4) Ibid

(5) Ibid

(6) Ibid

(7) "Blind Senator Has Friend and Guide as He Goes About Streets," *Newark Advocate and American Tribune,* January 9, 1928, p 3

(8) "Sees For His Master," *Mason City Globe and Gazette,* December 27, 1928, p 16

(9) Ascarelli p 36

(10) Ibid

(11) Ibid p 41

(12) Ibid p 50

(13) La Salle Kennels brochure, circa 1935

(14) "Trainer of Dogs to Guide Blind Arrives in City," *Los Angeles Times,* August 26, 1929, p 2A

Chapter 2: Joseph W. Jones

(1) "Mississippi History Now," Mississippi Historical Society

(2) Ibid

(3) United States Census, 1900

(4) Joseph W. Jones, Sr. Speech to the 1948 IAM Grand Lodge Convention

(5) *Machinists Monthly Journal,* November, 1946 p311

(6) Jones 1948 convention speech

(7) Ibid

(8) Ibid

(9) Ibid

(10) Ibid

(11) Ibid

Sidebar

(1) Joseph W. Jones, Sr. Speech to the 1948 IAM Grand Lodge Convention

Chapter 3: Guiding Eyes

(1) Machinists *Monthly Journal,* May, 1946, p124

(2) *"War Dogs: The Birth of the K-9 Corps,"* by Dr. Arthur W. Bergeron, Jr., U.S. Army Military History Institute, February 14, 2008

(3) Machinists *Journal,* May, 1946, p124

(4) Ibid

(5) Ibid

(6) Machinists *Monthly Journal,* November, 1946, p 311

(7) Minutes of the Meeting of the IAM Executive Council, September 26 – October 10, 1946, p 42

(8) Machinists Journal, November, 1946, p311

(Weather for October 1, 1946: Weather Underground: "History for Washington, DC, Tuesday, October 1, 1946" www.wunderground.com)

Sidebar

(1) Machinists *Monthly Journal,* November, 1946, p 311

Chapter 4: Moving West

(1) Machinists *Monthly Journal,* July, 1947 p270

(2) Joseph W. Jones, Sr., speech to IAM Grand Lodge Convention, Grand Rapids, MI, September, 1948

(3) Ibid

(4) Ibid

(5) "Agreement For The Training of Guide Dogs For The Blind," December 29, 1948

(6) Ibid

(7) Report of Inspector K.C. Rogers to Department of Professional and Vocational Standards, November 18, 1948

(8) James A. Arnerich letter to Dorothy Scott, March 22, 1949

(9) Kenneth E. Lynch letter to Dorothy Scott, April 8, 1949

(10) Ibid

(11) Committee report to State Board of Guide Dogs For The Blind, Dorothy Scott, April 26, 1949

(12) Ibid

Chapter 5: The Dream Becomes a Reality

(1)   Machinists *Monthly Journal*, June, 1949 p230

(2)   Joseph W. Jones, Sr., speech to IAM Grand Lodge Convention, Kansas, City, MO, September, 1952

(3)   Ibid

(4)   Ibid

(5)   Ibid

(6)   Ibid

(7)   Ibid

(8)   Machinists *Monthly Journal*, November, 1950 p345

(9)   Joseph W. Jones, Sr., speech to IAM Grand Lodge Convention, Kansas, City, MO, September, 1952

Chapter 6: Transitions

(1)   Joseph W. Jones, Sr., speech to IAM Grand Lodge Convention, San Francisco, CA, September, 1956

(2)   Ibid

Chapter 7: A New Home

(1)   International Guiding Eyes, Inc. brochure

(2)   *The Valley News* (Van Nuys, CA), April 9, 1961, p14A

(3)   *The Valley News* (Van Nuys, CA), October 24, 1967, p15

(4)   *The Valley News* (Van Nuys, CA), March 5, 1968, p7

(5)   *The Machinist*, February 26, 1970, p5

Sidebar – Heidi Banks

(1)   *Independent Press Telegram* (Long Beach, CA), January 14, 1968, p102

Chapter 8: Growing Pains

(1)   "Benefit Helps Group Get Money for Guide Dogs" *The Valley News* (Van Nuys, CA), July 26, 1973, p 13

(2)   "Novice Dog Instruction Scheduled," *The Valley News* (Van Nuys, CA), January 12, 1974, p 29

(3)   "Donation Aids Guiding Eyes," *The Valley News* (Van Nuys, CA), November 29, 1973, p 17

(4)   "Even Dogs Can Help," *The Valley News* (Van Nuys, CA), January 9, 1975, p4A

(5)   Bud Melvin interview, Patrick S. Halley, March 14, 2012

(6)   Ibid

(7)   *The Machinist,* December, 1978, p5

Chapter 9: Rebound

(1)   George Kourpias interview, Patrick S. Halley, December 3, 2011

(2)   M.E. "Bud" Melvin interview, Patrick S. Halley, December 8, 2011

(3)   Ibid

(4)   "Guiding Eyes' dog crusade opens," *The Machinist*, December, 1981, p5

(5)   M.E. "Bud" Melvin interview, Patrick S. Halley, December 8, 2011

(6)   IAM Grand Lodge Convention Proceedings, 1984, p261

(7)   IAM Grand Lodge Convention Proceedings, 1988, p118

Chapter 10: Guide Dogs of America

(1)   IAM Grand Lodge Convention Proceedings, 1992, p148

(2)   Ibid, p149

(3)   Ibid, p150

Acknowledgements

I wish to acknowledge and thank the following people who were helpful in creating this book: First and foremost, Dale Hartford, for his time, patience and support as we waded through the various drafts and issues. Rhonda Bissell and Chuck Jordan who were quick to respond to my many inquiries and requests; IAM General Vice President Bob Martinez and Susan Holmes from his staff for research at the Georgia State University Southern Labor Archives; Dr. Maurice Cunningham of the University of Massachusetts for research guidance; Patricia Kessler for her outstanding proxy research at the University of Wyoming American Heritage Center; Alan Peters of Can Do Canines and the Master Eye Foundation, and the Sinykin family, for invaluable information about the early days of the guide dog movement in America; Bill Upton of the IAM Communications Department for granting me unprecedented access to their trove of archived photographs; Shane Williams of Prestige Audio Visual and Creative Services for assistance in enhancing photographs that were nearly a century old; and Gary Otten for contributing original photography.

Finally, I wish to thank our creative team: Adele Pollis and Rich Chiarella of AP Associates for design, picture enhancements and editing; and Bill Burke of Page One Photography for his outstanding work, including pressing his own dog into service.

Photo Credits

Cover: Image from Guide Dogs of America archives

Foreword: Bill Burke, Page One Photography

Introduction: Bill Burke, Page One Photography

Page 2: Bill Burke, Page One Photography

Page 3: University of Wyoming American Heritage Center, Captain Lambert A. Kreimer Collection – Image enhancement courtesy of Prestige Audio Visual and Creative Services, Inc.

Page 4: University of California, Keystone-Mast Collection

Page 5: Lowell-Milken Foundation

Page 7: Courtesy of Sinykin Family, the Master Eye Foundation and Can Do Canines

Page 9: Lowell-Milken Foundation

Page 11: IAM archives

Page 12: University of Wyoming American Heritage Center, Captain Lambert A. Kreimer Collection

Page 13: Courtesy of Sinykin Family, the Master Eye Foundation and Can Do Canines; University of Wyoming American Heritage Center, Captain Lambert A. Kreimer Collection

Page 14: IAM archives

Page 18: IAM archives

Page 19: Courtesy of Shrine Auditorium; IAM archives

Page 20: IAM archives

Page 22: IAM archives, IAM archives

Page 23: IAM archives

Page 24: GDA archives; IAM archives; IAM archives

Page 25: IAM archives; IAM archives

Page 26: GDA archives; IAM archives

Page 27: GDA archives

Page 28: GDA archives

Page 29: IAM archives

Page 30: IAM archives

Page 31: GDA archives

Page 32: GDA archives

Page 33: GDA archives; GDA archives; GDA archives

Page 34: GDA archives

Page 35: GDA archives; IAM archives

Page 36: GDA archives; GDA archives

Page 37: GDA archives

Page 38: GDA archives; IAM archives

Page 39: GDA archives

Page 40: GDA archives

Page 41: GDA archives, GDA archives; GDA archives; GDA archives

Page 42: GDA archives; GDA archives; GDA archives

Page 43: IAM archives

Page 44: IAM archives; IAM archives

Page 45: GDA archives; GDA archives

Page 46: GDA archives

Page 47: GDA archives; GDA archives

Page 48: GDA archives; GDA archives

Page 49: GDA archives; GDA archives

Page 50: IAM archives; IAM archives

Page 51: IAM archives

Page 52: IAM archives

Page 53: IAM archives; IAM archives

Page 55: GDA archives

Page 56: GDA archives

Page 57: GDA archives; GDA archives; GDA archives; GDA archives

Page 62: GDA archives; GDA archives; GDA archives

Page 63: GDA archives; GDA archives; GDA archives

Page 64: IAM archives; GDA archives

Page 65: GDA archives

Page 66: GDA archives; GDA archives; GDA archives

Page 67: GDA archives; GDA archives

Page 68: GDA archives; GDA archives; GDA archives

Page 69: GDA archives; IAM archives; GDA archives

Page 70: GDA archives

Page 71: GDA archives; GDA archives; GDA archives; GDA archives

Page 72: GDA archives; IAM archives

Page 73: IAM archives

Page 74: IAM archives; GDA archives

Page 76: GDA archives; GDA archives; GDA archives

Page 77: GDA archives; GDA archives; GDA archives

Page 78: IAM archives

Page 79: GDA archives

Page 80: IAM archives; GDA archives

Page 81: GDA archives; IAM archives

Page 83: GDA archives

Page 84: GDA archives

Page 85: IAM archives; GDA archives; GDA archives; GDA archives; GDA archives

Page 86: GDA archives; GDA archives

Page 87: IAM archives; GDA archives

Page 88: GDA archives; GDA archives; GDA archives

Page 89: GDA archives; GDA archives

Page 90: GDA archives; GDA archives

Page 91: GDA archives; GDA archives

Page 92: GDA archives

Page 94: GDA archives; GDA archives

Page 95: GDA archives; GDA archives

Page 97: GDA archives

Page 98: GDA archives; IAM archives

Page 99: IAM archives; IAM archives

Page 100: GDA archives; IAM archives

Page 101: Bill Burke, Page One Photography

Page 102: Bill Burke, Page One Photography; Bill Burke, Page One Photography

Page 103: Bill Burke, Page One Photography; Bill Burke, Page One Photography; Bill Burke, Page One Photography

Page 104: IAM archives

Page 105: IAM archives

Page 106: IAM archives

Page 107: GDA archives; GDA archives; GDA archives; GDA archives

Page 108: GDA archives; GDA archives; GDA archives

Page 109: GDA archives; GDA archives

Page 110: GDA archives; GDA archives; GDA archives

Page 111: GDA archives; GDA archives; GDA archives

Page 112: GDA archives; IAM archives; GDA archives; IAM archives; IAM archives; GDA archives

Page 113: Bill Burke, Page One Photography

Page 114: Bill Burke, Page One Photography

Page 115: Bill Burke, Page One Photography; GDA archives; GDA archives; GDA archives

Page 116-117: Bill Burke, Page One Photography

Page 118-119: Bill Burke, Page One Photography

Page 120: Bill Burke, Page One Photography; Bill Burke, Page One Photography; Bill Burke, Page One Photography

Page 121: Bill Burke, Page One Photography

Page 122: Bill Burke, Page One Photography

Page 123: GDA archives; Bill Burke, Page One Photography

Page 124: Bill Burke, Page One Photography

Page 125: Bill Burke, Page One Photography

Page 126: Bill Burke, Page One Photography; Bill Burke, Page One Photography; Bill Burke, Page One Photography

Page 127: Bill Burke, Page One Photography; Bill Burke, Page One Photography

Page 128: Bill Burke, Page One Photography

Page 129: Bill Burke, Page One Photography

Page 130: Bill Burke, Page One Photography

Page 131: Bill Burke, Page One Photography

Page 132: GDA archives; Bill Burke, Page One Photography

Page 133: GDA archives; GDA archives

Page 134: GDA archives; GDA archives

Page 135: GDA archives; GDA archives

Page 136: GDA archives

Page 137: GDA archives; GDA archives

Page 138: GDA archives; GDA archives; GDA archives

Page 139: GDA archives; GDA archives; GDA archives

Page 140: Patrick S. Halley; Patrick S. Halley; Patrick S. Halley

Page 141: Bill Burke, Page One Photography

Page 143: Bill Burke, Page One Photography

Page 144: GDA archives; GDA archives; GDA archives

Page 145: Bill Burke, Page One Photography

Page 146: Bill Burke, Page One Photography

Page 147: GDA archives; GDA archives; GDA archives

Page 148: Bill Burke, Page One Photography; Bill Burke, Page One Photography

Page 149: Bill Burke, Page One Photography; Bill Burke, Page One Photography

Page 151: Bill Burke, Page One Photography

Page 152: Bill Burke, Page One Photography

Page 153: Bill Burke, Page One Photography

Page 154: Lorri Bernson collection; Lorri Bernson collection

Page 157: Lorri Bernson collection; Lorri Bernson collection

Page 158: Bill Burke, Page One Photography

Page 160: IAM archives

Page 161: IAM archives; IAM archives

Page 162: GDA archives; GDA archives; GDA archives

Page 163: GDA archives; GDA archives; GDA archives

Page 164: GDA archives; GDA archives; GDA archives; IAM Western Territory

Page 166: Courtesy of Gary Otten; Courtesy of Gary Otten

Page 167: IAM Western Territory; Courtesy of Gary Otten

Page 168: Courtesy of Garry Otten; Courtesy of Gary Otten

Page 169: GDA archives; Courtesy of Weldon Granger

Page 170: Courtesy of Morton Family; Courtesy of Weldon Granger

Page 171: Courtesy of Morton Family

Page 172: Bill Burke, Page One Photography

Page 174: GDA archives, enhancement courtesy of Prestige Audio Visual and Creative Services, Inc.; GDA archives; GDA archives

Page 175: IAM archives; GDA archives; IAM archives

Page 176: GDA archives; GDA archives; GDA archives

Page 177: GDA archives

Page 178: GDA archives; GDA archives

Page 179: GDA archives

Page 180: GDA archives; GDA archives

Page 181: GDA archives; GDA archives; GDA archives

Page 182: GDA archives; GDA archives; GDA archives

Page 183: Patrick S. Halley

Page 184: Bill Burke, Page One Photography

Page 185: Bill Burke, Page One Photography; Bill Burke, Page One Photography

Page 186: Bill Burke, Page One Photography; Bill Burke, Page One Photography

Page 187: Bill Burke, Page One Photography; Bill Burke, Page One Photography

Page 188: Bill Burke, Page One Photography; Bill Burke, Page One Photography; Bill Burke, Page One Photography

Page 189: Patrick S. Halley; Bill Burke, Page One Photography; Bill Burke, Page One Photography

Page 190: Bill Burke, Page One Photography

Page 191: Bill Burke, Page One Photography; Bill Burke, Page One Photography

Page 192: Bill Burke, Page One Photography; Bill Burke, Page One Photography

Page 193: Courtesy of the Morton Family; GDA archives

Page 194: GDA archives; GDA archives; GDA archives

Page 195: GDA archives; GDA archives; GDA archives

Page 196: Bill Burke, Page One Photography

Index

Guide Dogs of America Staff, December, 2011.